For Common Schools, Business Colleges, and the Counting House.

PRACTICAL

BOOK-KEEPING,

CONTAINING THOROUGH INSTRUCTION IN

Journalizing, Posting, and Closing,

TOGETHER WITH

PRACTICAL FORMS FOR WHOLESALING OR JOBBING, RETAILING, AND COMMISSION BY DOUBLE ENTRY: ALSO, REMARKS UPON NEGOTIABLE PAPER, FORMS FOR BUSINESS PAPER, ETC.

BY W. A. DREW,

Proprietor of Drew's Business College, Chicago.

CHICAGO:

GEO. SHERWOOD & CO.

Entered, according to the Act of Congress, in the year 1873, by
GEO. SHERWOOD & CO.,
in the Office of the Librarian of Congress, at Washington.

PREFACE.

In presenting this work to the public, our only apology is the public demand for a work on Double Entry Book-Keeping, so simplified that it can be taught by any teacher competent to teach a common school.

There is no good reason why Book-Keeping should not be taught in our common schools, as one of the most important and useful branches of education. As a mathematical drill for the student, it is equal to Algebra or Geometry, and as for its utility, no education is complete without it.

All the works on Book-Keeping heretofore published, fail to impart to the student a knowledge of Journalizing. Journalizing is the Alphabet of Accounts, and must be thoroughly learned before satisfactory progress can be made in this science.

There is an increasing demand on the part of the public, to have Double Entry Book-Keeping taught as one of the principal branches in our common schools. The attempts made heretofore have not been rewarded with satisfactory results, owing to the want of a text book that would teach the first principles. The author has made this work as progressive as possible, and the language used in giving rules for Journalizing, Posting, and Closing, is as plain and simple as the English language will permit. The practical forms for Wholesaling and Retailing are given, and it is believed that when the student understands those, he could adopt others, as occasion requires.

Single Entry is not introduced, for the reason that if the student understands Double Entry, he knows all about Single Entry. He has something deeper, viz: the principles of Debit and Credit that underlie the whole science of Accounts.

This work will be found adapted to common schools, business colleges, and the counting house; and if the author, after twenty years' labor, has succeeded in issuing a work the public demands, he feels confident that his labor will be appreciated.

He is willing and anxious to rest its merits with the public and trust to its good judgment for the introduction and perusal of this work.

W. A. Drew.

CONTENTS.

Contents.

INTRODUCTION.

Before the student enters upon the study of Book-Keeping, he should investigate the following explanations, and should become familiar with the following questions and answers, that he may have a better understanding of the work to be accomplished :

Q. What is Book-Keeping?

A. Book-Keeping is the science of Accounts.

Q. What does Book-Keeping teach?

A. It teaches the most practical forms for keeping and preserving a history of business transactions.

Q. How many distinct methods are there for keeping books?

A. Two. Single and Double Entry.

Q. How many practical forms are there?

A. Almost every kind of business has a form adapted to that peculiar business, although the principles of Debit and Credit never vary.

Q. What should every accountant do?

A. He should give a full and correct history of his business transactions, and select a form that is practical for his business.

Q. How is the accountant to know what form to select?

A. His own judgment, or the judgment of others having more experience, should be consulted.

Q. Define Single and Double Entry?

A. In Single Entry a debit or credit is made for every business transaction. In Double Entry, every business transaction produces both a debit and credit of equal amount, in the Journal and Ledger.

Q. What other advantages has Double Entry over Single?

A. In Single Entry we have no proof of the work, and as there are no Expense or Profit and Loss Accounts, we have no correct record of the gains and losses in business.

In this work the student is introduced to Double Entry at first, and when he has a knowledge of this method, he will understand Single Entry.

Q. How many principal books are used in Single Entry?

A. Two. Day Book and Ledger.

Q. How many principal books are kept in Double Entry?

A. Three. Day Book, Journal, and Ledger. When a history is given in the Journal, only two are used, Journal and Ledger.

Q. What does the Day Book by Double Entry show?

A. A history of the business transactions not entered in the Cash Book.

Q. What does the Journal show, or express?

A. It expresses the debit and credit of the Day Book entries under Ledger titles.

Q. What is the Ledger?

A. It is the reservoir of accounts.

Q. Into what book do accounts flow, that are recorded in the Day Book?

A. Into the Journal, and those that have cash as part payment, are carried to the Cash Book.

Q. Into what book do entries flow from the Journal?

A. Into the Ledger.

Q. What is the Cash Book used for?

A. To keep a correct history of the cash received and paid out.

Q. Into what book do the entries flow from the Cash Book?

A Into the Ledger.

Q, What are the Auxiliary Books?

A. The various helping books, among which are the Cash Book, Invoice Book, Sales Book, Check Book, Order Book, Bank Pass Book, etc., the kind and number depending upon the nature of the business.

ABBREVIATIONS AND CHARACTERS.

Acct. or a/c	Account.
Am't.	Amount.
Bal.	Balance.
B. B.	Bill Book.
bbls.	Barrels.
Bills Pay.	Bills payable.
" Rec.	" receivable.
Bot.	Bought.
bu.	Bushels.
¢	Cents.
Cap.	Capital.
C. B.	Cash Book.
Co.	Company.
Cr.	Credit.
C. S. B.	Commission Sales Book.
D. B.	Day Book.
Dr.	Debit.
ds.	Days.
E. O. E.	Errors and omissions excepted.
gal.	Gallons.
hhd.	Hogshead.
I. B.	Invoice Book.
Inst.	Instant.
Inv't.	Inventory.
lbs.	Pounds.
L. F.	Ledger Folio.
Mdse.	Merchandise.
Paymt.	Payment.
%	Per. cent.
Prem.	Premium.
S. B.	Sales Book.
Ship't.	Shipment.
Sunds.	Sundries.
yds.	Yards.
√	Check mark.
$	Dollars.

RULES AND EXERCISES IN JOURNALIZING.

RULE 1.—Debit what you receive, what you buy, what comes into your possession, or what costs you value.

RULE 2.—Credit what you sell, what you pay out, what goes out of your possession, or what produces you value.

The following business transactions, representing Day Book entries, will furnish exercises for the student in journalizing.

No Ledger will be introduced till the student becomes proficient in journalizing. It is from this exercise the student gets a knowledge of the principles of debit and credit. Journalizing is the key to Book-keeping, and should be thoroughly understood before posting to the Ledger.

SET 1, NO. 1.

Chicago, Jan. 1, 1872.				
Bot. of Geo. Jones,				
5 bbls. flour, at $10	50	00		
Paid him cash in full			50	00

The following entry will give the student an idea of the form :—

1st.

Mdse	50	00		
To Cash			50	00

The date should be made on the line between the entries, the same as the Day Book entries. The student should be careful and carry out the amount of the debit entries in the debit column and the credit entries in the credit column. This rule is not observed in the exercise for journalizing, as no debits or credits are expressed. In the Journal, the first entry and first column is the debit entry and Dr. column, and the second entry and second column the credit entry and Cr. column. The student can refer to the Journal in this work for the form.

Chicago, Jan. 2, 1872.				
Sold Wm. Brown, 4 bbls flour, at $11	44	00		
Recd. in paymt. cash			44	00
3.				
Bot. of John Smith, 7 bbls. flour, at $10 $70 5 bbls. pork, " $15 $75	145	00		
Paid him cash in full			145	00
4.				
Bot. of R. Good, 10 bbls. beef, at $12 $120 50 doz. brooms, " 2 100 20 bbls. pork " 15 300	520	00		
Paid him cash			520	00
5.				
Bot. of Geo. Davis, House and lot on West Madison Street, for	5000	00		
Paid him cash			5000	00
The Journal entry will be, Real Estate	5000	00		
To Cash			5000	00
We debit real estate when we buy it, give it credit when we sell it, and the difference will show our gain or loss on real estate.				
6.				
Sold Wm. Lyman, A vacant lot on West Madison Street for	2800	00		
Recd. in paymt., 200 bbls. flour, at $10 $2000 40 bbls. pork, " 20 800			2800	00

CHICAGO, JAN. 6, 1872.				
Bot. of J. Russell, A vacant lot on West Harrison St.	250	00		
Paid him 20 bbls. pork, at $12.50			250	00
9.				
Sold Geo. G. Jones, 50 bbls. pork, at $25 $1250 100 " flour, " 12.50 1250	2500	00		
Recd. in paymt., 25 shares C. B. and Q. R. R. Stock, at $100			2500	00
C. B. and Q. R. R. Stock	2500	00		
To Mdse.			2500	00
10.				
Bot. of H. Johnson, 4 shares Commercial Bank Stock, at $100	400	00		
Paid him 40 bbls. flour, at $10			400	00
15.				
Sold John Goss, 2 shares Com'l Bank Stock, at $100	200	00		
Rec'd. cash			200	00
18.				
Sold W. A. Drew, 25 bbls. flour, at $12	300	00		
Recd. in paymt., 3 shares N. Y. Cen. R. R. Stock, at $100			300	00
22.				
Bot. of Geo. Davis, 100 bu. wheat, at $1.25	125	00		
Paid him cash			125	00

Chicago, Jan. 23, 1872.				
Sold John Smith, 10 shares C. B. and Q. R R. Stock, at $100	1000	00		
Recd. in paymt. cash			1000	00
24.				
Sold R. Good, 20 doz. brooms, at $2.50	50	00		
Recd. in paymt. cash			50	00
25.				
Bot. of James Williams, 5 shares 1st Nat. Bank Stock at $100	500	00		
Paid him 5 shares C. B. and Q. R. R. Stock, at $100			500	00
26.				
Sold James Boyd, 5 shares Nat. Bank Stock, at $100	500	00		
Rec'd. in paymt. cash			500	00
27.				
Bot. of Geo. Jones, for cash, 400 bu. corn. at 25c.	100	00		
30.				
Sold Samuel Thompson, 400 bu. corn, at 30c.	120	00		
Rec'd. in paymt., 12 bbls. flour, at $10			120	00

Set 1, No. 2.

PROMISSORY NOTES.

Q. What is a promissory note?

A. A promissory note is a written or printed promise to pay a certain sum of money at a specified time, or on demand.

Q. Who is the maker of a promissory note?

A. The person who signs it or makes the promise.

Q. Who is the payee?

A. The payee is the person to whom the note is made payable.

Form for a Promissory Note.

$500.

Chicago, April 24th, 1873.

Sixty days after date I promise to pay John Smith or order five hundred dollars, with interest at ten per cent. per annum. Value received.

Geo. Jones.

Q. Who is the maker of the above promissory note?

Q. Who is the payee?

Q. When I speak of John Smith's note, do I refer to John Smith's property or John Smith's promise to pay a certain sum of money?

A. John Smith's promise. In speaking of these notes we should always describe them as the maker's note, not a note on the maker or received from the maker.

Q. When you receive another person's note, what do you debit?

A. Debit Bills Receivable.

Q. When you sell or dispose of another person's note, what do you credit?

A. I credit Bills Rec.

Q. When you give out or issue your note what do you credit?

A. I credit Bills Payable.

Q. When you receive your note, or when it comes back into your possession, what do you debit?

A. I debit Bills Payable.

After having committed the foregoing rules to memory, the student should journalize the following exercises in No. 2.

SET 1, NO. 2,

CHICAGO, FEBRUARY 1, 1872.				
Bot. of Wm. Lyman,				
10 bbls. flour, at $10	100	00		
Paid him my note for			100	00
Mdse.	100	00		
To Bills Pay.			100	00
2.				
Sold Geo. Webb,				
5 bbls. flour, at $12	60	00		
Rec'd. in paymt. his note for			60	00
"				
Geo. Davis paid me cash for his note for	150	00	150	00
In the above entry the student must debit Cash and credit Bills Receivable, bearing in mind that every debit must have a credit, which must be expressed in the Journal.				
3.				
Bot. of Wm. Watson, on my note				
25 bbls. flour, at $10	250	00		
50 " beef, " $12	600	00	850	00
4.				
Paid A. H. Hull,				
Cash for my note	475	00		
5.				
Bot. of R. H. Hamlin, for cash,				
W. W. Wright's note, for	785	00		

CHICAGO, FEBRUARY 6, 1872.				
Sold C. P. Smith & Co.,				
W. W. Wright's note for	785	00		
Recd. in paymt.,				
70 bbls. flour, at $10 — $700				
100 bu. rye, " 85¢. — 85			785	00
8.				
Bot. of R. Davis,				
House and lot on West Harrison Street, for	3000	00		
Paid him John Smith's note for			2000	00
R. Good's note			1000	00
Real Estate	3000	00		
To Bills Rec			3000	00
9.				
Paid Charles Jones cash for my note, for			800	00
10.				
Sold Wm. Fox,				
House and lot on West Harrison Street, for	3500	00		
Recd. in paymt.,				
His note for			3000	00
A. W. Anthony's note for balance			500	00
15.				
Exchanged notes with Hart, Jones & Co., receiving their note in exchange for mine, amounting to	1500	00		
16.				
Paid cash for my note,				
Wm. Watson's favor	850	00		

CHICAGO, FEBRUARY 17, 1872.				
Sold Scott & Co.,				
100 bu. wheat, at $1.00	100	00		
Recd. in paymt. my note,				
Wm Lyman's favor			100	00
20.				
Bot. of D. Baldwin,				
5 shares C. B. & Q. R. R. Stock,				
at $100	500	00		
Paid him my note at 10 ds. for			300	00
My note at 30 ds. for			200	00
22.				
Sold Geo. West,				
3 shares C. B. & Q. R. R. Stock,				
at $110	330	00		
Recd. in paymt. cash			330	00
23.				
Bot. of Wm. Wells,				
Samuel Boyd's note for	220	00		
Paid him 2 shares C. B. & Q. R. R.				
Stock, at $110			220	00
25.				
Recd. of Hart, Jones & Co.,				
My note in exchange for theirs for	1500	00	1500	00

SET 1, NO. 3.

RULES FOR JOURNALIZING SUNDRY ITEMS.

The word sundries, as applied to book-keeping, has reference to different species of property.

If I buy corn and oats I have bought sundry items, but not sundry species of property, as corn and oats would be merchandise; but if I buy wheat and John Smith's note, I have bought sundry species of property, and should debit Mdse. and Bills Receivable.

The same rule will apply to the credits.

Entries for Practice.

Chicago, March 1, 1872.				
Sold Wm. Watson,				
10 bbls. pork, at $10	100	00		
Recd. in paymt., cash			50	00
His note for			50	00
The Journal entry should be Sunds. To Mdse.				
The following is the form: —				
Sunds. To Mdse.			100	00
Cash	50	00		
Bills Rec.	50	00		
2.				
Sold John Goss,				
25 bbls. flour, at $10 — $250				
20 " pork, " 20 — 400			650	00
Recd. in paymt., cash	300	00		
His note for balance	350	00		
3.				
Bot. of S. C. Goodrich,				
15 bbls. flour, at $10	150	00		
Paid him my note for			100	00
Cash			50	00
4.				
Sold Geo. Parker,				
500 bu. wheat, at $1.10	550	00		
Recd. in paymt., cash			300	00
Geo. Davis' note			200	00
20 bbls. apples, at $2.50			50	00
When more than one species of property is received and more than one disposed of in the same entry, the Journal entry should be headed "Sunds. To Sunds." On the same line first write the debit Sunds. and then drop one line and in the credit column write the credit Sunds.				

CHICAGO, MARCH 5, 1872.				
Bot. of Chas. Jones,				
500 bu. corn, at 40¢. $200				
800 " wheat, at $1.00 800			1000	00
Paid him John Goss' note for	350	00		
Cash	300	00		
My note for balance	350	00		
6.				
Bot. of H. C. Curtis,				
House and lot on West Randolph Street, for	2700	00		
1200 bu. corn, at 40¢.	480	00		
Paid him cash			500	00
My note for balance			2680	00
6.				
Sunds. To Sunds.				
Real Estate	2700	00		
Mdse.	480	00		
Cash			500	00
Bills Pay.			2680	00
8.				
Sold Jones & Co.,				
1200 bu. corn, at 42¢.	504	00		
4 shares 1st Nat. Bank Stock, at $100	400	00		
Recd. in paymt., cash			500	00
Their note for $200				
A. C. Hall's note for 204			404	00
10.				
Bot. of Geo. Hoffman,				
A farm in La Salle Co., containing 80 acres, at $10	800	00		
Paid him cash			400	00
My note			300	00
100 bu. wheat, at $1.00			100	00
13.				
Paid R. C. Leonard cash for W. M. Brown's note	450	00		

CHICAGO, MARCH 15, 1872.				
Paid H. C. Curtis for my note, amounting to	2680	00		
Paid him Jones & Co.'s note			500	00
Cash			1500	00
6 shares New York Cen. R. R. Stock			600	00
My note for balance			80	00
18.				
Sold James Fisk,				
80 acres of land in La Salle Co., at $15	1200	00		
50 shares E. R. R. Stock, at $50	2500	00		
Recd. in paymt. his note for			3700	00
23.				
Paid Geo. Bond,				
Cash for my note	400	00		
" John Smith's note	500	00	900	00
24.				
Bot. of W. O. Drew,				
400 bu. oats, at 25¢ $100				
500 " rye, " 50¢ 250	350	00		
A vacant lot on State Street, for	1500	00		
6 shares C. R.I. R. R. Stock, at $100	600	00		
Paid him my note for			450	00
Cash			1000	00
Potter Palmer's note			500	00
500 bu. wheat, at $1.00			500	00

SET 1, NO. 4.

BILLS OF EXCHANGE OR DRAFTS.

A Draft or Bill of Exchange is an order to pay a specified sum of money. A foreign draft is called a bill of exchange. Custom has established the commercial term of drafts for bills drawn and paid in the United States.

The person who makes or signs the order is called the drawer.

The person to whom the draft is addressed is called the drawee.

The person to whom it is made payable is called the payee.

If "A" orders "B" to pay "C," A is the drawer, B is the drawee, and C the payee.

FORM FOR A DRAFT.

$500 Chicago, April 28th, 1873.

At ten days' sight pay Charles Jones or order five hundred dollars, and charge to the acct. of

W. A. DREW.

To Davis & Howe,
450 Broadway, New York.

Q. Who is the drawer of the above draft?

Q. Who is the drawee?

Q. Who is the payee?

RULE 1.

When you draw a draft on a person you should credit that person.

RULE 2.

When a person draws a draft on you, debit that person.

CHICAGO, APRIL 1, 1872.				
Bot. of Scott & Co.,				
700 bu. wheat, at $1.25	875	00		
Paid them my draft on Wheeler & Wilson for			875	00
Mdse.	875	00		
To Wheeler & Wilson			875	00
2.				
Paid Geo. Jones cash for Wm. Lyman's draft on me for	250	00		
Wm. Lyman	250	00		
To cash			250	00
3.				
Paid Johnson & Co., for C. B. Howard & Co.'s draft on me for	1500	00		
Paid 1500 bu. corn, at 50¢			750	00
Cash			700	00
My note for balance			50	00

CHICAGO, APRIL 4, 1872.				
Bot. of H. O. Freeman & Co.,				
7 shares City Bank Stock, at $100	700	00		
Paid them my draft on Geo. Jones			300	00
My note for			200	00
Cash			150	00
5 bbls. flour, at $10			50	00

RULE 3.

When you receive or purchase a draft drawn on other parties, you should debit Bills Receivable.

A draft is a bill receivable when it passes from the hands of the drawer.

RULE 4.

When you sell or dispose of a draft drawn by other parties, you should credit Bills Receivable.

CHICAGO, APRIL 6, 1872.				
Sold Hall & Davis,				
450 bu. rye, at 50¢	225	00		
Received their draft on the 2d National Bank for			225	00
8.				
Sold A. P. Andrews, for cash, the draft I recd. of Hall & Davis, for	225	00		
9.				
Bot. of A. H. Hinman,				
A Bill of Mdse. as per invoice, amounting to	1250	00		
Paid him my draft on C. P. Smith & Co., for			900	00
My draft on L. Friend, for			300	00
Cash			50	00

A sight draft is one that is payable at sight.

A time draft is payable at specified time after sight.

When you accept a draft, you write "accepted" across the face of it, also your name and date of acceptance.

Your acceptance becomes a Bill Payable, as it is your promise in writing to pay the amount of the draft.

RULE 5.

When you accept a draft, you debit the person that draws on you and credit Bills Pay.

CHICAGO, APRIL 15, 1872.				
Accepted Scott & Co.'s draft on me at 5 ds. for	475	00		
16.				
Sold John Wilson,				
200 bbls. flour, at $9	1800	00		
James Davidson's draft on Scott & Co. for	2000	00		
Recd. in paymt., cash			1000	00
Jones & Co.'s draft on me for			2000	00
Geo. Whitney's draft on me for			400	00
My note for			400	00
20.				
Accepted H. Williams' draft on me at 10 ds. for			600	00
H. Williams	600	00		
To Bills Pay.			600	00
"				
Paid cash for my acceptance, Scott & Co.'s favor			475	00
24.				
Bot. of D. Baldwin,				
5 shares Mich. So. R. R. Stock, at $100	500	00		
Paid him my draft on G. Harris for			250	00
My note for			75	00
Geo. Jones' note for			100	00
Wm. Lyman's draft on John Fox for			75	00

CHICAGO, APRIL 30, 1872.				
Paid cash for my acceptance, H. Williams' favor, amounting to	600	00		

SET 1, No. 5.

PERSONAL ACCOUNTS.

Accounts kept with persons are called personal accounts.
You debit a person when he costs you value.
You credit a person when he produces you value.

RULE 1.

When you buy of a person on account, credit him.

RULE 2.

When you sell to a person on account, debit him.

RULE 3.

When you pay a person on account, debit him.

RULE 4.

When a person pays you on account, credit him.

CHICAGO, MAY 1, 1872.				
Bot. of James Williams, on acct. 75 bbls. apples, at $2	150	00		
2.				
Sold Charles Downs, on acct., 400 bu. oats, at 25¢	100	00		
700 " corn, " 50¢	350	00	450	00
4.				
Paid Wm. Gordon cash on acct.	145	25		

CHICAGO, MAY 6, 1872.				
Recd. of James Davidson,				
Cash on acct.	75	00		
8.				
Bot. of A. C. Dewey,				
750 bu. barley, at 60¢	450	00		
Paid him cash			250	00
Balance on acct.			200	00
9.				
Bot. of R. H. Drew,				
500 lbs. maple sugar, at 15¢	75	00		
Paid him cash			25	00
My note for			25	00
Balance on acct.			25	00
10.				
Accepted A. Bailey's draft on me for the balance due him on acct., for	435	00		
11.				
Paid J. McMillan on acct., with my draft on W. A. Drew, for	725	50		
J. McMillan	725	50		
To W. A. Drew			725	50
13.				
Tracy & Co. paid me on acct., with their draft on Wm. Wells for	70	00		
Their note for	50	00		
Cash	100	00	220	00
15.				
Geo. Davis paid me on acct. with my note for	180	35		

Chicago, May 20, 1872.				
Paid A. Bailey for my acceptance for	435	00		
Paid my draft on R. H. Drew for			75	00
My note for			200	00
Cash for balance			160	00
22.				
Bot. of Geo. Folson,				
400 bu. corn, at 30¢	120	00		
Chas. Burnham's note for	73	28		
Paid him my draft on A. C. Druitt for			145	00
Cash			48	28
23.				
Paid Edwd. Bates for my note, amounting to	1675	00		
Paid him my draft on Wm. Curtice for			1000	00
My note for			600	00
Cash			15	00
Balance on acct.			60	00
24.				
Accepted G. Fisher's draft on me at 10 ds. for	125	00		
28.				
Paid John Smith cash on acct.	95	00		
30.				
Recd. of Tracy & Co., Their note for bal. due me on acct.	450	00		

Set 1, No. 6.

INTEREST AND DISCOUNT.

Interest represents a sum paid by the borrower to the lender for the use of money.

RULE 1.

Debit interest whenever you pay anything for the use of money or lose by it.

Interest should always be debited on Bills Payable.

RULE 2.

Credit interest whenever you receive anything for the use of money or whenever you gain by it.

Credit interest on Bills Receivable.

The student must not get the idea that he receives or pays interest but receives or pays for interest, or for the use of money; and whatever he receives or pays for the use of money should be debited or credited.

CHICAGO, JUNE 1, 1872.				
Paid Wm. Allen cash for my note and interest				
Face of note	100	00		
Interest	10	00		
Sunds. To Cash			110	00
Bills Pay.	100	00		
Interest	10	00		
In the above entry, Interest costs value, and should be debited.				
2.				
Recd. of David Jones, Cash for his note and interest			495	00
Face of note	450	00		
Interest	45	00		
The Journal entry should be Cash To Sunds. The sunds. are Bills Rec. and Interest. No account is made with interest till it is received or paid.				
3.				
Sold David West, 100 bbls. flour, at $8	800	00		
Recd. in paymt. my note for			500	00
Interest due on note			50	00
His note for balance.			250	00

CHICAGO, JUNE 4, 1872.				
Paid R. Wilson for my note for	480	00		
Interest on note	48	00		
Paid him cash			480	00
6 bbls. flour, at $8			48	00
5.				
Bot. of John Long,				
50 bbls. flour, at $7			350	00
Paid him cash	150	00		
My note for	125	00		
Balance on a/c	75	00		
Discount is the deduction made for the payment of money before it is due. Discount, like interest, should be debited whenever you lose by it, and credited whenever you gain by it.				
10.				
Discounted in Drew's College Bank, C. H. King's note for	500	00		
Recd. cash, less discount			490	00
Discount off			10	00
Sunds. To Bills Rec.			500	00
Cash	490	00		
Discount	10	00		
15.				
Discounted my note, Geo. Jones' favor, for	250	00		
Paid cash, less discount			247	50
Discount off			2	50
Bills Pay. To Sunds.	250	00		
Cash			247	50
Discount			2	50
16.				
Sold Wm. Watson,				
250 bu. wheat, at $1			250	00
Recd. in paymt. his draft on John Smith for	150	00		
Cash	100	00		

CHICAGO, JUNE 17, 1872.				
I have drawn a draft on Wm. Lyman for the balance due me on acct., and discounted the same in the 1st Nat. Bank.				
Amount of draft	350	00		
Recd. cash			346	50
Discount on draft			3	50
19.				
Sold J. McMillan,				
75 bbls. apples, at $2.50	187	50		
Recd. C. Howard's note, at 5% disct.				
Face of note			100	00
Discount on note	5	00		
Cash			92	50
Credit Mdse. and Dis. and debit Bills Rec. and cash.				
20.				
Sold James Druitt, on a/c, at 30 ds.				
400 bu. wheat, at $1.20	480	00		
22.				
James Druitt has this day discounted the bill due me for Mdse., amounting to	480	00		
Recd. cash			456	00
Discount off			24	00
Cr. James Druitt.				
30.				
Bot. of Chas. Boyd,				
His draft on C. P. Smith & Co., for at 5% discount.	150	00		
Paid cash			142	50
Discount off			7	50

SET 1, NO. 7.

PREMIUM, EXPENSE, AND PROFIT AND LOSS ACCOUNTS.

RULE 1.

When you pay more for a draft or bill of exchange than its face you debit Premium.

RULE 2.

When you receive more for a draft than its face you credit Premium.

RULE 3.

When you lose you debit Profit and Loss.

RULE 4.

When you gain you credit Profit and Loss.

RULE 5.

When you pay out anything to carry on your business at the store, you debit Store Expense. When you pay for any expense for your family, you debit Family Expense. When you pay out anything for your personal expense, you should debit Personal Expense. You can, however, keep the full expense account under the head of Expense if you do not wish to keep separate expense accounts.

CHICAGO, JULY, 1, 1872.				
Paid Cash for rent of Store Room, One month in advance,			75	00
2.				
Bot. of Geo. Thompson for Cash, His Dft. on Smith & Rising, at 2 % discount.				
Face of Draft,	500	00		
Paid cash less discount.			490	00
Discount off,			10	00
3.				
Paid cash for a Gas Bill, for gas consumed at my private residence,				
Amounting to	10	50		

CHICAGO, JULY 5, 1872.				
Bot. of Geo. Wells,				
1400 bu. Corn, at 30¢	420	00		
Paid him my draft on Howard & Co., N. Y., at 2% Discount.				
Face of draft			420	00
Discount off	8	40		
Paid cash for balance			8	40
Debit Mdse and Discount.				
6.				
Paid John Jones on a/c with my draft on Geo. Davis, at 5% premium.				
Face of draft	100	00		
Premium	5	00	105	00
8.				
Bot. of Howard & Co., their draft on J. J. Astor, at 3% premium.				
Face of draft	400	00		
Premium	12	00		
Paid cash			300	00
My draft on C. P. Smith & Co., for balance			112	00
9.				
Paid cash for Groceries, purchased of Riale Bros.	25	00		
12.				
Paid cash for a new suit of Clothes for my personal use	60	00		
18.				
John Smith owes me on his note	250	00		
Having failed he has paid me 50% on a dollar.				
Received cash			125	00
Lose the balance			125	00

CHICAGO, JULY 20, 1872.				
H. Williams owes me on a/c He having become insolvent and absconded, I lose the whole debt	70	00	70	00
22.				
Found a pocket-book containing a sum of money, and having advertised the same, have not found the owner. I have invested the same in my business, amounting to	475	00		
23.				
The thieves broke into my store last night and carried off Mdse. valued at	250	00		
26.				
Geo. Goodrich has called at my store and given proof that the money found on the 22d inst., belonged to him. I have paid him the full amount	475	00		
28.				
The thieves that broke open my store have been arrested, and Mdse. recovered amounting to	170	00		

SET I, NO. 8.

SHIPMENT OR CONSIGNMENT ACCOUNTS.

RULE I.

When you ship goods to be sold on your account and risk, you make shipment to the place you send them Dr. for the full cost of the Mdse. and charges, and credit what you ship or what produces the shipment.

CHICAGO, AUGUST 1, 1872.				
Shipped to Johnson & Webb, Buffalo, to be sold on my a/c and risk,				
2500 bu. corn, at 25¢	625	00		
1500 " wheat, at $1	1500	00	2125	00
3.				
Shipped to Scott & Co., N. Y., to be sold on my a/c and risk,				
2500 bu. wheat, at $1	2500	00		
Paid cash for insurance	25	25		
			2525	25
5.				
Bot. of John Goss, with my note, and shipped to Wright & Gibbs, Toledo, to be sold on my a/c and risk,				
5000 bu. corn, at 25¢	1250	00		

An account sales of a shipment is a statement of the sales, charges and net proceeds. The total sales are called the gross sales, the balance after the charges are deducted is called the net proceeds.

RULE 2.

When you receive an account sales of a shipment, and the person to whom you made the shipment sends only the account sales and does not remit to you, you debit him, for he has the net proceeds of your shipment. If he remits, debit what you receive and credit the shipment.

15.				
Recd. from Johnson & Webb, Buffalo, an acct. sales of my shipment of the 1st inst. They have remitted their draft on the First Nat. Bank for the net proceeds, amounting to	2500	00		

Chicago, Aug. 16, 1872.				
Received cash for the draft on the First National Bank,	2500	00		
17.				
Received of Scott & Co., New York, an acct. sales of my shipment to them on the 3d inst. Net proceeds due on a/c,	2750	00		
20.				
Bot. of Foster & Wells, Buffalo, on account, and shipped the same to Scott & Co., N. Y., to be sold on my acct. and risk, 250 barrels of flour, at $10,	2500	00		
Shipment from Buffalo to N. Y. To Foster & Wells				
22.				
I have drawn a draft on Scott & Co., New York, for the balance due me on acct. and discounted the same in Drew's College Bank				
Face of draft	2750	00		
Recd. cash for proceeds of draft			2722	50
Discount on draft			27	50
25.				
Received intelligence that my shipment from Buffalo to N. Y. was destroyed by fire in the warehouse of Scott & Co. The shipment not being insured, the total loss amounts to	2500	00		

Chicago, August 26, 1872.				
Bot. of Armour, Dole & Co. on acct.				
2750 bu. corn, for	675	00		
Paid cash for insurance on the same	6	75	681	75
Mdse. To Sunds.	681	75		
Armour, Dole & Co.			675	00
Cash			6	75
29.				
Bot. for cash of Johnson & Blake, N. O., and shipped the same to Boston, to be sold on my account,				
27,500 lbs. of cotton, at 15¢	4125	00		
Paid cash for drayage	10	00	4135	00
Shipt. from N. O. to Boston	4135	00		
To Cash			4135	00
31.				
Paid Armour, Dole & Co., on acct.,				
Cash	350	00		
My draft on J. Jones for	200	00	550	00

Set 1, No. 9.

STOCK AND PARTNERSHIP ACCOUNTS.

The Stock Account used in Double Entry Book-keeping represents the resources and liabilities of the person doing business.

On opening a set of books a statement should be made, giving a list of the resources and the liabilities.

Rule 1.

In journalizing the resources, debit the property on hand and the persons that owe you, and credit Stock for the full amount.

Journalize the following entries :—

Chicago, Sept. 1, 1872.				
I invested cash in business amounting to	2500	00		
Cash	2500	00		
To Stock			2500	00

CHICAGO, SEPT. 2, 1872.				
Inventory of my resources.				
Mdse. as per inventory	1500	00		
Cash on hand	700	00		
Geo. Wilson owes me on a/c	250	00		
Amos King on his note	300	00	2750	00

RULE 2.

In journalizing the liabilities or debts, debit Stock for the full amount of your liabilities, and credit the persons that you owe and Bills Pay. for the amount due on your note.

The student must bear in mind that Resources, Effects or Assets represent your property and what is due you; and Liabilities, your debts.

If the Resources exceed the Liabilities, the difference or balance is called Net Capital. If the Liabilities exceed the Resources, the balance is called Net Insolvency.

3.				
I owe on commencing business				
John Long on a/c	75	00		
David Watson on my note	150	00		
Chas. Jones on a/c	200	00	425	00
5.				
Inventory of my resources,				
Cash	3000	00		
Bills Rec. as per Bill Book	700	00		
W. W. Wright owes me on a/c	50	00		
Samuel Davis " " "	60	00	3810	00
"				
LIABILITIES.				
I owe J. Graves on a/c	72	00		
W. Goodrich "	100	00		
Geo. Goldsmith on my note $500				
Joseph Friedman on my note 200	700	00	872	00

RULE 3.

When two or more persons enter into partnership, make a statement of the resources invested in the firm by each partner; and if the liabilities of either partner are assumed by the firm, debit each partner for the amount thus assumed, and credit the persons that he owes, and Bills Pay. for the amount of notes outstanding.

RULE 4.

When a member of the firm puts in or invests resources in the firm, he should be credited.

RULE 5.

When a member of the firm draws out resources from the firm for his private use, debit him.

RULE 6.

When the firm assumes the payment of the private debt of either member of the firm, debit that member.

John Smith and Wm. Lyman have this day entered into partnership in the Dry Goods and Jobbing Business, under the firm of Smith & Lyman, parties to share equally in gains and losses.

CHICAGO, SEPT. 25, 1872.				
John Smith invested Bills Rec., as per Bill Book	1400	00		
6 shares C. B. & Q. R. R. Stock, at $100	600	00		
Mdse. as per inventory	2000	00		
John Fox owe's him on acct.	500	00		
Cash	500	00	5000	00
"				
Wm. Lyman invested				
Real Estate	1500	00		
10 shares 1st Nat. Bank Stock, at $100	1000	00		
Bills Rec. as per Bill Book	1500	00		
Cash	500	00	4500	00

CHICAGO, SEPT. 25, 1872.				
John Smith's liabilities assumed by the firm,				
Due Howard & Co., on a/c	700	00		
Chas. Kendall, on his note	25	00		
E. Drew, on a/c	50	00	775	00
"				
Wm. Lyman's liabilities,				
Due E. Richards, on a/c	65	00		
A. H. Kendall, on his note	100	00	165	00

QUESTIONS FOR REVIEW.

What is Book-keeping?

How many methods are there for keeping books?

Explain the difference between Single and Double Entry.

How many principal books are kept by Single Entry?

How many by Double Entry?

Do you keep a Journal by Single Entry?

In what book do you express the Debits or Credits by Single Entry?

In what book do you express the Debits and Credits by Double Entry?

What is the Ledger?

What is the first rule for Journalizing?

Repeat rule second.

Suppose you buy wheat of John Smith and pay cash, how would you journalize the entry?

Suppose you sold wheat to Geo. Jones, and received cash. Journalize the entry.

Journalize the following entries:

Sold Wm. Watson for cash a House and Lot.
Bot. 2 Shares C. B. & Q. R. R. Stock, and paid flour.
Sold John Smith 500 Bush. Corn for cash.

The teacher can drill the classes in mental Journal entries, exercising his ingenuity in putting the questions to the student. The author of this work has adopted this method of giving mental Journal entries for the past ten years in his business colleges with the most satisfactory results.

REVIEW OF NO. 2. SET 1.

What is a Promissory Note?

Under what Ledger titles do you express these notes?

What is a Bill Rec.?

What is a Bill Pay.?

When you receive another person's note, what do you debit?

When you dispose of this note, what do you credit?

When you give out your own note, what do you credit?

When you receive back or redeem your note, what do you debit, and what do you credit?

A. I debit Bills Pay. and credit whatever I pay in exchange for the note.

If you buy corn of D. Lyman and pay your note, what is the Journal entry?

Rec. Cash for John Smith's note. Journalize the entry.

Paid cash for your own note.

Paid cash for Geo. Jones' note.

Received John Smith's note in exchange for yours.

Bot. a farm and paid your note.

No. 3. Set I

EXERCISES IN JOURNALIZING—CONTINUED.

Bot. corn, paid cash and your note.

Sold rye, recd. cash and John Lyman's note.

Bot. corn and oats, paid cash, your note, and Amos King's note.

Sold house and lot and Commercial Bank Stock. Rec. in paymt. cash, your note, and Wm. Ross' note.

No. 4. Set I.

What is a Draft or Bill of Exchange?

Who is the drawer of a draft?

Who is the drawee?

Who is the payee?

Whom do you credit when you draw a draft on a person?

What do you do when a person draws on you?

What do you debit when you receive or purchase a draft drawn by A on B?

A. I debit Bills Rec.

What do you credit when you sell a draft drawn by A on B?

What is a Sight Draft?

What is a Time Draft?

How do you accept a draft?

When you accept a draft, do you make a promise in writing to pay it?

What does your acceptance become to you?

A. A Bill Pay.

Accepted John Jones' draft on you at ten days. Journalize the entry.

Paid cash for your acceptance.

Bot. corn and paid your draft on Jones & Co., for the same.

Paid Wm. Allen cash for Joseph Friedman's draft on you.

Sold Geo. Hoffmann Mdse. Rec. in Paymt. his draft on Davis & Co.

The teacher can add to the list of mental exercises given here if the student requires them.

No 5. Set 1.

What are Personal Accounts?

When do you debit a person?

When do you credit a person?

Whom do you credit when you buy of a person on account?

When you sell to a person on account, what do you do?

When you pay a person on account?

When a person pays you on account?

Bot. flour of John King on account.

Paid John Smith cash on account.

Geo. Jones paid you on account with his note.

Bot. Sugar of Wm. Goss, paid him cash, your note and the balance due on account.

Paid W. A. Drew on account with your order on C. Curtis.

No. 6. Set 1.

What is Interest?

What is Principal?

When do you debit Interest?

On what bills do you debit Interest?

On what bills do you credit Interest?

Remark.—When you buy a note and pay for or make an allowance for the interest due on the note at the time of purchase, you debit interest on Bills Receivable. In all other cases credit interest on Bills Rec.

What is Discount?

When do you debit Discount?

When do you credit Discount?

Paid cash for your note and interest. Journalize the entry.

Rec. cash for A. Stone's note and interest.

Discounted Wm. Wells' note in the bank. Received cash less discount.

Discounted your note, C. Williams' favor, paid cash less discount.

No. 7. Set 1.

When do you debit Premium?

When do you credit Premium?

When do you debit Profit and Loss?

When do you credit Profit and Loss?

When do you debit Store Expense?

When do you debit Family Expense?

When do you debit personal expense?

The teacher can add to the list of mental entries on Nos. 7, 8 and 9, similar to those given on the preceding numbers in this work.

No. 8. Set 1

When you ship goods to be sold on your own account and risk, what is the rule for Journalizing the entry?

What is an account sales of a shipment?

When you receive only an account sales of a shipment, whom do you debit?

When the consignee remits cash with the account sales, what do you do?

A. Debit cash and credit the shipment.

No. 9. Set 1

What does the Stock Account represent?

What is necessary to do when you open a set of books?

A. Make a statement of the resources and liabilities in the Day Book or Journal.

NEGOTIABLE PAPER.

By negotiable paper is meant, evidence of debit which may be transferred by indorsement or delivery, so that the holder may sue the same in his own name. Among the list and the most common in use, are promissory notes, bills of exchange, bank checks, etc.

If A gives B his note payable to B or bearer, B can sell it to C by delivery, but if A promises to pay B or order, B must indorse the note to transfer it to C; that is B must write his name on the back of the note. B's name is his order for A to pay C or bearer, then C could collect from A, but if A was unable to pay, then C could collect from B. If B, however, had written after his signature the words "without recourse," then C would lose the value of the note if he could not collect from A.

If B indorses A's note, he promises to pay it if A does not, and if B, C and D indorse A's note and E holds the note at maturity, E would look to A, the maker, first, then to B, then to C, in the order in which the indorsements were made. Every person who indorses a note promises to pay it, if the maker and previous indorsers fail, unless he writes the words "without recourse," which releases the indorser from payment of the note. E could not, however, collect A's note from the first indorser B, until he had used all legal means to collect from A; and the statutes in most of the States require written notice to be given the indorsers if the maker does not pay at maturity, or the indorsers are not holden, for the law supposes that if B pays A's note, that he should receive due notice that the maker has not paid it at maturity, that he may have an opportunity to collect from A, the maker, if resources can be found belonging to him.

A draft varies from a promissory note in this respect: There is a direct promise by the maker of the note to pay the payee or his order, or to bearer, while the drawer of a draft makes an indirect promise to pay the payee, only on condition that the drawee does not.

If A draws a draft on B in favor of C, and B dishonors it by refusing to pay it, then A would be holden for the amount and C could collect the amount of draft from A, together with the costs, but if A ordered B to pay C, and B accepts the draft by writing "accepted" across the face together with date and signature, then B would be holden to C for the payment of the draft at maturity, and if C could not collect from B, then he would have recourse on A. The drawer of an accepted draft is holden for payment, on the same conditions as the first indorser of a promissory note.

If A promises to pay B a sum of money, and does not insert the words, or order, or bearer, the note is not negotiable.

A promissory note may be written on paper or a good substitute for it, with ink or pencil, in any language. There is no special form required by law; but to make a perfect promissory note, it should be written on paper, with ink, in a plain hand. It should be dated, and the sum written in the body of the note. The figures, corresponding with the amount in writing, should be made at the left hand corner at the top. It should specify when it is to be paid, and the rate per cent. for interest, and if to be paid at any particular place, it should be mentioned in the note.

A promissory note will not draw interest unless so specified. If, however, it is not paid when due, it will draw the legal rate from that time till the final settlement.

The legal rate of interest is that established by law, which varies in different States. If the note specifies that it is to draw interest and no rate is mentioned, it will draw the legal rate only.

When more than the legal rate is collected it is called usury. There is a penalty for collecting usury in all the States but California. This varies in different States, from the forfeiture of the interest to the whole debt and interest. The legal rate in Illinois is six per cent. when no rate is mentioned, but as high as ten per cent. is legal if specified in the note.

All time paper has three days of grace in all the States but California; but when the third day comes on Sunday, or a legal holiday, it is due on the second day of grace.

If there are indorsements to a promissory note, the holder should present it for payment, when due, at the maker's place of business, during business hours, and if not paid by the maker when due, written notice should be sent to the indorsers. If payable at a particular place, as at a bank or an office, the note should be left there for collection, and written notice sent to the maker when the note matures. It would be well to observe the same rules if there were no indorsers, but the rules of the law are more exact on the subject of negotiable paper where there are indorsers than those of any other department of Mercantile Law.

A check on a bank should be presented as soon as convenient, say on the day it is received or the day following. Bank checks are seldom accepted by the bank, but they are often certified by the teller, who writes "good" on the check, over his signature, which binds the bank for the payment of the same.

The student having acquired the principles of Debit and Credit from the exercises in Journalizing, can now proceed to Journalize the following transactions which we will call the Day Book or memoranda of the business.

Check with this mark (√) on the left of the Day Book entries after journalizing, to avoid omissions.

DAY BOOK.

Set 2, No. 1.

Chicago, Jan. 1, 1873.				
I have this day invested cash in business amounting to	500	00		
2.				
Paid cash for rent of store room, one month in advance	25	00		
3.				
Bot. of Geo. Jones for cash,				
20 bbls. flour, at $4.25	85	00		
12 bbls. beef, at $11.25	135	00		
5 bbls. pork, at $8	40	00	260	00
5.				
Sold John Smith for cash,				
20 bbls. flour, at $5	100	00		
12 bbls. beef, at $12.50	150	00	250	00
8.				
Bot. of Wm. Watson on a/c,				
75 bbls. pork, at $9	675	00		
15 bbls. beef, at $11	165	00	840	00
12.				
Sold Geo. Williams on a/c,				
25 bbls. pork, at $10	250	00		
10 " beef, " 12.50	125	00	375	00

Chicago, Jan. 13, 1873.				
Bot. of Wm. Simpson,				
120 bbls. flour, at $4.50	540	00		
Paid him cash			300	00
Balance on a/c			240	00
15.				
Sold David Jenkins,				
50 bbls. pork, at $10	500	00		
20 " flour, " 5	100	00	600	00
Recd. in paymt., cash $450				
Balance on a/c 150				
16.				
Sold James Wells, on his note,				
50 bbls. flour, at $5 $250				
5 " beef, " 12 60	310	00		
18.				
Bot. of Geo. Johnson, on my note,				
20 bbls. beef, at $9	180	00		
4 " pork, " 8	32	00	212	00
20.				
Sold R. Lewis, for cash,				
20 bbls. beef, at $10	200	00		
25.				
Recd. of David Jenkins,				
Cash on acct.	150	00		
"				
Paid Wm. Simpson, on acct.,				
40 bbls. flour, at $6	240	00		
Cash	200	00	440	00

CHICAGO, JAN. 30, 1873.

Paid Geo. Johnson cash for my note	212	00		
"				
Inventory of Mdse. on hand, 9 bbls. beef, at $8 $72 10 bbls. flour, at $5 50 $122				

JOURNAL.

NO. 1, SET 2.

CHICAGO, JAN. 1, 1873.

63	Cash	500	00		
63	To Stock			500	00
	2.				
63	Store Expense	25	00		
63	To Cash			25	00
	3.				
64	Mdse.	260	00		
63	To Cash			260	00
	5.				
63	Cash	250	00		
64	To Mdse.			250	00
	8.				
64	Mdse.	840	00		
64	To Wm. Watson			840	00

CHICAGO, JAN. 12, 1873.

64	Geo. Williams	375	00		
64	To Mdse.			375	oc
	13.				
64	Mdse. To Sunds.	540	00		
63	Cash			300	00
64	Wm. Simpson			240	00
	15.				
64	Sunds. to Mdse.			600	00
63	Cash	450	00		
65	David Jenkins	150	00		
	16.				
65	Bills Rec.	310	00		
64	To Mdse.			310	00
	18.				
64	Mdse.	212	00		
65	To Bills Pay.			212	00
	20.				
63	Cash	200	00		
64	To Mdse.			200	00
	25.				
63	Cash	150	00		
65	To David Jenkins			150	00
	26.				
64	Wm. Simpson To Sunds.	440	00		
64	Mdse.			240	00
63	Cash			200	00
	30.				
65	Bills Pay.	212	00		
63	To Cash			212	00

POSTING TO LEDGER.

The student having Journalized No. 1. Set 2, can now proceed to post the same to the Ledger.

Posting is grouping, or collecting the accounts. All the Debits of Mdse. expressed in the Journal must be posted to the debit side of this acccount in the Ledger, and the Credits of Mdse. on the credit side of the Mdse. Account. The same rule will apply to all the other accounts. First open an account with Stock in the Ledger, and as Stock is credited by cash in the Journal, we post to the credit side of Stock, "By Cash $500," entering the page of the Ledger in the Journal, and checking in the Journal the page of the Ledger. Next in the index under the Letter S, write the word Stock, and the page on which the Stock Account is found in the Ledger. Next open an account with Cash in the Ledger, and debit it "To Stock," and note in the index the page of the Cash Account. Index every new account opened in the Ledger.

The next account that appears in the Journal is the Expense Account. As we have no Expense Account open in the Ledger, we open one and debit it "To Cash," and credit Cash by Expense.

After the student has posted all the accounts found in the Journal for this number, he can proceed to take the first Trial Balance; that is, add the debits and credits of all unbalanced accounts in the Ledger. The object in taking the first Trial Balance is to ascertain if the Ledger is in balance, or in other words, if we have an equal amount of debit and credit in the Ledger. If the Ledger is in balance, it is good evidence that our work is correct, but not positive proof. Either of the following errors could be committed and still obtain the first Trial Balance:

1. Incorrect Journalizing.
2. Posting to wrong accounts.
3. Neglecting to post all the accounts.

The experienced accountant is not apt to post to the wrong account, but more liable to post to the wrong side of the account, or omit to post the right amount of debit or credit, which would throw the Ledger out of balance. If the Ledger is out of balance it cannot be closed; furthermore, it is certain there is a mistake which must be looked up. Students may at first find some difficulty in detecting the error, if the Ledger does not balance, but as a prominent feature of learning to keep accounts, is learning to look up and correct errors, the student should learn how to detect them.

First examine your additions; be sure you have made no mistake in footing up your accounts in the Ledger, or in footing the total Ledger accounts. If assured that the additions are correct, check from the Journal to the Ledger, making a dot with a pencil on the line where each account is posted. After having checked all the entries in the Ledger, examine in detail all the accounts posted to the Ledger, and if there are entries posted not checked, erase the figures only, and thus proceed till the first Trial Balance is obtained. The pencil marks in the Ledger should be erased with a rubber. Neatness is indispensable to a good accountant. The teacher should insist that the work be neatly done.

If the work is posted correctly the following Trial Balance will be obtained. The student should carry out the balances as shown in the form. He can copy this in the Journal and refer to it when making out a balance sheet. All ruling should be made in red ink, and red ink should be used where *italics* occur in this work.

FIRST TRIAL BALANCE FOR NO. 1, SET 2.

JANUARY 1873.	Face of Ledger.				Balances.			
	Dr.		*Cr.*		*Dr.*		*Cr.*	
Stock			500	00			500	00
Cash	1550	00	997	00	553	00		
Store expense	25	00			25	00		
Merchandise	1852	00	1975	00			123	00
Wm. Watson			840	00			840	00
Geo. Williams	375	00			375	00		
Wm. Simpson	440	00	240	00	200	00		
Bills Rec.	310	00			310	00		
	4552	00	4552	00	1463	00	1463	00

CLOSING THE LEDGER.

Having obtained the correct Trial Balance, the student can close the Ledger.

By closing we obtain a condensed statement of our financial standing at the time, which, compared with the statement made at the time of opening our books, will show our gain or loss in business.

We will first open an account representing our gains and losses, which we will call Profit and Loss Account, and WE WILL TRANSFER OUR LOSSES TO THE DEBIT OF PROFIT AND LOSS, AND OUR GAINS, TO THE CREDIT OF PROFIT AND LOSS. We will open an account, to which we will transfer our Resources and Liabilities, which we will call the Balance Account, and WILL TRANSFER ALL THE RESOURCES TO THE DEBIT OF BALANCE AND THE LIABILITIES TO THE CREDIT OF BALANCE. The student should thoroughly understand the above instructions before proceeding to close, for he should not only know how to do it, but why he does it.

Next bring the amount of unsold property on the credit of the account it represents. In this set the unsold property is Mdse., amounting to $122.

On the credit of the Mdse. Account in the Ledger, with red ink, we make the entry "By Bal. Inv. $122," and transfer this amount to the debit of Balance, because Mdse. unsold is a resource, and make the entry in black ink, "To Mdse. Inv.," $122. Should there be other species of property on hand, proceed in the same way.

We will, for the present, leave Stock unclosed, for the reason that the balance of stock represents our Net Capital, and we wish to increase or decrease it with our gains or losses in business.

Now close the first account after Stock, which is Cash.

The debit of Cash shows the amount of cash on hand when we commenced business, together with what we have received since.

The credit of Cash shows the amount of cash paid out. The difference or balance, must show the amount on hand, which is entered on the credit of Cash in red ink, "By Balance," and transferred to the debit of Balance in black ink "To Cash." The inventory and closing entries should be made in red ink.

In transferring these amounts, the student should remember, the balances are always transferred in black ink to the opposite side from the closing entry in red ink. This brings the balance on the same side as before the transfer, as the closing entry is the excess of the larger side. The Bal. of Cash, $553.00 shows a resource, or amount on hand, and should be transferred to the debit of Balance.

Next in order comes Expense Account.

The debit of an Expense Account shows the expense of the business. In this No., it is $25, the amount paid for store rent, and represents a loss, which is transferred to the debit of Profit and Loss.

The debit of Mdse. shows what Mdse. has cost us, or what we paid for it.

The credit shows the sales of Mdse., or what it has produced us.

We must add the unsold Mdse. to the sales, and the balance will show a gain or loss. As it produced $245 more than it cost us, we must come to the conclusion we have made $245 on Mdse., which must be transferred to the credit of Profit and Loss.

Wm. Watson's account is next in order.

He has a credit by Mdse., showing that we purchased that amount of him on account, and as he has no debit, the balance being $840, a liability, must be transferred to the credit of Balance, making the entry, "To Balance," in red ink, on the debit of his account, and by "Wm. Watson" on the credit of Balance, in black ink.

Geo. Williams owes us $375 for Mdse. sold him on the 12th. This sum shows a resource, which should be transferred to the debit of Balance.

Wm. Simpson owes us $200 on account, which shows a resource, and we transfer to the debit of Balance from the credit of Wm. Simpson's account.

David Jenkins' account balances, and as we have no resource or liability in his account, we close the account.

The debit of Bills Rec. Account, shows bills or notes received. The credit would show the amount of Bills Rec. sold.

The balance should always show the amount of notes on hand. In this set it amounts to $310, which is a resource, and should be transferred to the debit of Balance.

The credit of Bills Payable Account, shows the amount of our notes issued. The debit, our notes redeemed. The Balance, the amount outstanding. This account balances, having redeemed with cash the note issued for Mdse.

Having closed all the accounts in the Ledger but Stock, Profit and Loss, and Balance, we now proceed to take the second Trial Balance, which will prove that we have transferred the correct Balances. The second Trial Balance is the amount of debits and credits of the unclosed accounts. The following is the result:

Stock			500	00
Profit and Loss	25	00	245	00
Balance	1560	00	840	00
	1585	00	1585	00

This Trial Balance is not recorded.

Should there be partners, bring them into the second Trial Balance.

We will now close Profit and Loss into Stock. By inspection, we find the loss amounts to $25, and the gains to $245; making a net gain of $220.

By examination of the Stock Account, we find that we had a Net Capital of $500 when we opened the books, and having a net gain of $220, we transfer from the debit of Profit and Loss, in red ink, to the credit of Stock, in black ink. Our Net Capital now amounts to $720. We now close Stock into Balance, transferring from the debit of Stock to the credit of Balance; making the entry, By Stock, in the Balance Account in red ink, as it shows our Net Capital and is the closing entry in the Balance Account.

It is hoped that our explanations of this No., have been so thorough and simple that the student will understand them, and be able to Journalize, post, and close No. 2 without difficulty.

The student will find a list of the resources on the debit of Balance, and liabilities on the credit of Balance; losses on the Dr. of Profit and Loss, and gains on the Cr. of Profit and Loss.

The student should now make out a Balance Sheet as shown in this work. This balance sheet is the most practical form of making a condensed statement of the business transactions, and can be made out at any time by taking an inventory of the unsold property, and the first Trial Balance.

If the student does not thoroughly understand posting, and closing this No., he will do well to go over the work again.

LEDGER INDEX.			
A.		**G.**	
B.		**H.**	
Bills Receivable,	65, 87	Hart, Jones & Co.,	88
" Payable,	65, 88		
Balance,	65, 90		
C.		**I. J.**	
Cash,	63, 86	Interest,	89
Carpenter, B. F.,	87	Jenkins, David,	65
Chapin & Jones,	89	Jones John,	88
D.		**K.**	
Day, Harvey,	89		
Discount,	89		
E.		**L.**	
F.		**M.**	
Field, Leiter & Co.,	88	Merchandise,	64, 87

LEDGER INDEX.

LEDGER.

No. 1, Set 2.

Dr. STOCK. *Cr.*

Jan.	31	*To Bal.*	65	720	00	Jan.	1	By Cash	54	500	00
						"	31	By Profit & Loss	63	220	00
				720	00					720	00

Dr. CASH. *Cr.*

Jan.	1	To Stock	54	500		Jan.	2	By Store Expense	54	25	00
"	5	" Mdse.	54	250	00	"	3	" Mdse.	54	260	00
"	15	" "	55	450	00	"	13	" "	55	300	00
"	20	" "	55	200	00	"	26	" Wm. Simpson	55	200	00
"	25	" D. Jenkins	55	150	00	"	30	" Bills Pay.	55	212	00
						"	31	" *Bal.*	65	553	00
				1550	00					1550	00

Dr. STORE EXPENSE. *Cr.*

Jan.	2	To Cash	54	25	00	*Jan.*	31	*By Profit & Loss*	65	25	00
				25	00					25	00

No. 1, Set 2.

Merchandise.

Dr.						*Cr.*				
Jan.	3	To Cash	54	260 00		Jan.	5	By Cash	54	250 00
"	8	" Wm. Watson	54	840 00		"	12	" G. Williams	55	375 00
"	13	" Sunds.	55	540 00		"	15	" Sunds.	55	600 00
"	18	" Bills Pay.	55	212 00		"	16	" Bills Rec.	55	310 00
"	31	" *Profit & Loss*	65	245 00		"	20	" Cash	55	200 00
						"	26	" W. Simpson	55	240 00
						Jan.	31	" *Bal. Invt.*	65	122 00
				2097 00						2097 00

Wm. Watson.

Dr.						*Cr.*				
Jan.	31	*To Bal.*	65	840 00		Jan.	8	By Mdse.	54	840 00

Geo. Williams.

Dr.						*Cr.*				
Jan.	12	To Mdse.	55	375 00		*Jan.*	31	*By Bal.*	65	375 00

Wm. Simpson.

Dr.						*Cr.*				
Jan.	26	To Sunds.	55	440 00		Jan.	13	By Mdse.	55	240 00
						"	31	" *Bal.*	65	200 00
				440 00						440 00

No 1, Set 2.

Dr. **David Jenkins.** *Cr.*

Jan.	15	To Mdse.	55	150	00	Jan.	25	By Cash	55	150	00

Dr. **Bills Receivable.** *Cr.*

Jan.	16	To Mdse.	55	310	00	*Jan.*	31	*By Bal.*	65	310	00

Dr. **Bills Payable.** *Cr.*

Jan.	30	To Cash	55	212	00	Jan.	18	By Mdse.	55	212	00

Dr. **Profit and Loss.** *Cr.*

Jan.	31	To Store Expense	63	25	00	Jan.	31	By Mdse.	64	245	00
"	"	*To Stock*	63	220	00						
				245	00					245	00

Dr. **Balance.** *Cr.*

Jan.	31	To Mdse. Invt.	64	122	00	Jan.	31	By Wm. Watson	64	840	00
"	"	" Cash	63	553	00	"	"	*By Stock*	63	720	00
"	"	" G. Williams	64	375	00						
"	"	" W. Simpson	64	200	00						
"	"	" Bills Rec.	65	310	00						
				1560	00					1560	00

BALANCE SHEET FOR No. 1, SET 2.

	L. Fol.	Face of Ledger.		Property Unsold.	Profit and Loss.		Stock.		Balance.	
		Dr.	*Cr.*		*Dr.*	*Cr.*	*Dr.*	*Cr.*	Resources.	Liabilities.
Stock	63		500 00					500 00		
Cash	63	1550 00	997 00						553 00	
Store Expense	63	25 00			25 00					
Merchandise	64	1852 00	1975 00	122 00		245 00			122 00	
Wm. Watson	64		840 00							840 00
Geo. Williams	64	375 00							375 00	
Wm. Simpson	64	440 00	240 00						200 00	
Bills Rec.	65	310 00							310 00	
		4552 00	4552 00	122 00						
To Stock for Net Gain					220 00			220 00		
					245 00	245 00				
To Balance for Net Capital							720 00			720 00
							720 00	720 00	1560 00	1560 00

EXPLANATION OF THE BALANCE SHEET.

First rule the border as shown for No. 1, and then rule the head lines, after which rule five more lines than you have accounts, for Stock, or seven, for two partners. The inventory should be entered in red ink, and transferred to the debit of Balance in black ink.

The Balance Sheet shows the same results as the Balance and Profit and Loss Accounts in the Ledger, viz: the Gains and Losses, and Resources and Liabilities. When there are many Personal Accounts unbalanced, the amounts are grouped in this way: All due the firm are Resources, and appear under "Personal Accounts due us;" and all that the firm owe are liabilities, which appear under "Personal Accounts that we owe." A Balance Sheet should be made out when the books are closed. The student should make out a Balance Sheet for sets 2, 3 and 4. He can refer to the Balance and Profit and Loss Accounts in his Ledger for the correct balances.

REVIEW OF THE LEDGER.

What does the Stock Account represent?

What does the Profit and Loss Account represent?

What does the Debit of the Profit and Loss Account show?

What does the Credit of the Profit and Loss Account show?

What does the Debit of the Balance Account show?

What does the Credit of the Balance Account show?

What does the Debit of the Cash Account show?

What does the Credit of the Cash Account show?

What does the Balance of the Cash Account show?

What does the Debit of the Bills Receivable Account show?

What does the Credit of the Bills Receivable Account show?

What does the Balance of the Bills Receivable Account show?

What does the Debit of the Bills Payable Account show?

What does the Credit of the Bills Payable Account show?

What does the Balance of the Bills Payable Account show?

What does the Debit of a Personal Account show?

What does the Credit of a Personal Account show?

What does the Balance of a Personal Account show?

What does the Debit of the Mdse. Account show?

What does the Credit of the Mdse. Account show?

What does the Inventory of the Mdse. Account show?

After the Inventory is added to the Credit side of the Mdse. Account what does the Balance between the Debit and the Credit show?

Where is the Balance of Cash transferred, and why?

Where is the Balance of the Bills Receivable Account transferred, and why?

Where is the Balance of the Bills Payable Account transferred, and why?

Can the Credit of the Cash Account be the largest? Tell why.

Into what Account do you close all Personal Accounts?

Interest closes into what Account, and why?

Premium closes into what Account, and why?

All Expense Accounts close into what Account, and why?

Shipment Accounts close into what Account, and why?

Give a list of all the Accounts that you can mention that close into Balance.

Give a list of all the Accounts that you can mention that close into Profit and Loss.

How often should Books, kept for the Retail Business, be closed?

How often should books, kept for the Wholesale Business, be closed?

What is the First Trial Balance, and what does it show?

How often should a First Trial Balance be taken in business?

Can you close the Ledger if out of Balance?

If your Ledger is out of Balance, what do you do?

What is the Second Trial Balance?

What do you do after you obtain the Second Trial Balance?

Into what account do you close Stock or the Partners?

Where do you find a list of your Resources?

Where do you find a list of your Liabilities?

Where do you find a list of your Losses?

Where do you find a list of your Gains?

Where do you find your Net Capital?

What does the Net Capital show?

If you add your Net Capital to your Liabilities, what will it balance?

If you subtract your Liabilities from your Resources, what will the balance show?

DAY BOOK.

SET 2, NO. 2.

CHICAGO, FEB. 1. 1872.				
Inventory of my resources on commencing business.				
Mdse. as per Inventory	2175	00		
Cash on hand	1650	00		
Wm. Marshall owes me on a/c	145	00	3970	00
LIABILITIES.				
Due James Williams on a/c	350	00		
W. A. Downs on my note	700	00	1050	00

CHICAGO, FEB. 3, 1872,

Sold Simpson & Mathews,				
14 hhds. sugar, 18900 lbs. at 6¢	1134	00		
9 " molasses, 1020 gals. at 25¢	255	00	1389	00
Recd. in paymt. cash $450				
Their note for 312				
" " " 338				
Balance on a/c 289				
8.				
Sold Drew & Hinman,				
9 hhds. molasses, 1530 gals.,				
at 30¢ $459				
18 bags coffee, 3200 lbs., at 8½¢ 272	731	00		
Recd. in paymt. cash			430	00
Their note at 30 days for bal.			301	00
10.				
Sold Stewart & Co.,				
25 bags coffee, 8800 lbs., at 8¢	704	00		
Recd. cash			354	00
Jas. Williams' draft on me for			350	00
12.				
Bot. of Smith & Rising,				
21 hhds. sugar, 25200 lbs., at 6¢	1512	00		
Paid them cash			450	00
Simpson & Mathews' note			312	00
My note for			750	00
15.				
Sold Geo. Drew,				
9 hhds. sugar, 12600 lbs. at 7½¢			945	00
Recd. cash	520	00		
His note for bal.	425	00		

CHICAGO, FEB. 20, 1872.				
Paid W. A. Downs for my Note for	700	00		
My order on Wm. Marshall			125	00
Drew & Hinman's note			301	00
Cash for balance			274	00
22.				
Bought of Wm. Marshall,				
9 hhds. sugar, 10300 lbs., at 6¢, $618				
14 " molasses, 1530 gal., at 20¢ 306	924	00		
Paid him cash			204	00
My note for			400	00
Bal. on a/c			320	00
24.				
Sold O. C. Hurd & Co.,				
4 hhds. sugar, 5150, lbs at 8¢ $412				
8 hhds. molasses, 510 gals., at 30¢, 153	565	00		
Recd. in paymt. cash			340	00
Bal. on a/c			225	00
26.				
Paid Wm. Marshall on a/c with my order on Simpson & Mathews for	125	00		
28.				
Sold Geo. Campbell on a/c,				
5 hhds. sugar, 5150 lbs. at 8¢	412	00		
Property on hand,				
Mdse. as per Inventory $960				

FIRST TRIAL BALANCE.

SET 2, NO. 2.

	Face of Ledger.				Balances.			
	Dr.		Cr.		Dr.		Cr.	
Stock	1050	00	3970	00			2920	00
Mdse.	4611	00	4746	00			135	00
Cash	3744	00	928	00	2816	00		
Wm. Marshall	270	00	445	00			175	00
Bills Pay.	700	00	1850	00			1150	00
" Rec.	1376	00	613	00	763	00		
Simpson & Mathews,	289	00	125	00	164	00		
O. C. Hurd & Co.	225	00			225	00		
Geo. Campbell	412	00			412	00		
	12677	00	12677	00	4380	00	4380	00

Net gain for February, $1095.00.

SET 2, NO. 3.

CHICAGO, MARCH 1, 1872.

Inventory of my resources:				
Cash in Citizens' Bank	750	00		
" on hand	657	00		
Mdse. as per Inventory	1073	00		
House and Lot on West Adams St.	3500	00		
John Smith owes me on his note	420	00		
H. Williams owes me on a/c	250	00	6650	00
LIABILITIES.				
I owe as follows:				
J. D. Grant on a/c	450	00		
Wm. Marshall on a/c	360	00		
John Jones on my note $120				
Snow & Johnson on my note 320	440	00	1250	00
2.				
Sold Riale Brothers,				
20 bbls. sugar, 6000 lbs. at 6¢ $360				
30 " molasses, 1230 galls.,				
at 30¢ 369	729	00		
Recd. in paymt., cash			279	00
J. D. Grant's order on me for			450	00

CHICAGO, MARCH 5, 1872.

Bot. of Snow & Johnson,				
60 bags of coffee, 9600 lbs. at 7½¢ $720				
15 chests tea, 600 lbs., at 45¢ 270	990	00		
Paid them cash			220	00
John Smith's note			420	00
Bal. on a/c			350	00
10.				
Bot. of J. D. Andrus & Co.,				
82 bbls. pork at $10	820	00		
Paid check on Citizens' Bank			225	00
3000 lbs. sugar at 6¢ $180				
410 gals. molasses, 30¢ 123			303	00
Bal. on a/c			292	00
13.				
Accepted Snow & Johnson's draft on me for	250	00		
15.				
Sold Joseph Friedman,				
1025 gals. molasses at 35¢ $358.75				
2000 lbs. sugar at 8¢ 160.00	518	75		
Recd. in paymt. my note			320	00
Cash for balance			198	75
17.				
Received John Wheeler's note in exchange for mine, for his accommodation, for	240	00		
20.				
Paid John Jones cash for my note	120	00		

Chicago, March 22, 1872.				
Sold Peter Cooper,				
1600 lbs. coffee at 10¢ $160				
200 " tea at 70¢ 140				
35 bbls. pork at $10 350	650	00		
Recd. in paymt. his note			250	00
Cash			200	00
Bal. on a/c			200	00
23.				
Paid Wm. Colwell cash for repairs on dwelling house on Adams Street	50	00		
24.				
Paid cash to Potter Palmer for rent of store room	125	00		
25.				
Sold H. C. Spencer for cash, a bill of Mdse. amounting to	625	00		
26.				
Paid cash for gas bill for store,	20	25		
27.				
Paid Wm. Marshall on a/c, with my				
draft on H. Williams for	250	00		
Cash	110	00	360	00
28.				
Recd. cash of Wm. Davis for rent of house on W. Adams St.			50	00
29.				
Sold Benton & Cord on their note				
200 lbs. tea at 70¢	140	00		
3200 " coffee at 10¢	320	00	460	00

Chicago, March 29, 1872.				
Property on hand.				
Mdse. as per Inventory	460	00		
Real Estate	3500	00	3960	00

The student should carry out the balances as shown for No. 1, in Set 2. Only the Ledger footings are given in this work.

First Trial Balance for March.				
Stock	1250	00	6650	00
Citizens' Bank	750	00	225	00
Cash	2009	75	645	25
Mdse.	2883	00	3285	75
Real Estate	3500	00	50	00
Bills Rec.	1370	00	420	00
" Pay.	440	00	930	00
Snow & Johnson	250	00	350	00
J. D. Andrews			292	00
Peter Cooper	200	00		
Expense	195	25		
	12848	00	12848	00
Net gain, $717.50.				

AUXILIARY BOOKS.

We will now introduce the student to the principal Auxiliary Books used in Book-keeping. The book most in use, and one that should be kept in every branch of business, is the Cash Book. The Cash Book should be used expressly for a history of the Cash transactions. The form will be given and explained hereafter.

THE SALES BOOK.

In this book we keep a record of the Sales of the Mdse., and it is used in Wholesaling and Jobbing. In Retailing, a history of the Sales is usually made in the Day Book, or Journal.

THE INVOICE BOOK.

In this book is written a copy of the bills of Mdse. purchased. In retailing however, the bills are usually placed on file, or pasted in some old account book, kept for that purpose.

THE BILL BOOK.

This book is used to keep a record or history of the Notes received and issued.

THE CHECK BOOK

is used for drawing or checking money out of the Bank, and where no Bank Account is kept, a record of the Checks and Deposits can be kept on the vouchers, taking a balance whenever a deposit is made, or a check drawn.

No. 1, Set 3 gives the first practical form for Wholesaling and Jobbing, and consists of a Bill Book, Invoice Book, Sales Book, Journal, and Ledger. No Day Book is kept, but a history given in the Journal and Auxiliary Books. The same form would be practical for Retailing, by keeping a history in the Journal, and dispense with the Sales and Invoice Books. Many of the best accountants dispense with the Day Book entirely. The Day Book given in Nos. 1, 2, and 3, is not a practical form for business, but is arranged for practice for the student. By writing the Day Book, the student acquires the correct method of giving a history of the business, and he will acquire the Practical Forms in Sets 3 and 4.

The following memoranda will be explained, and the student should write up all the books belonging to this Set, post the Journal and Cash Book to the Ledger, close, and make out a Balance Sheet.

Memoranda for Set 3, No. 1.

Chicago, April 1, 1872.				
I commenced this day in the Wholesale and Jobbing Grocery Business, with a Cash Capital of The above entry should be made on the Debit side of the Cash Book as shown in the Cash Book for this Set.	15000	00		

Chicago, April 2, 1872.

Bot. of Stewart & Son, on a/c at 10 ds.				
25 hhds. sugar, 27500 lbs., at 8¢	2200	00		
25 " molasses, 1675 gals., at 25¢	418	75	2618	75
Enter the above in the Invoice Book, and Journalize the entry in the Journal.				
3.				
Sold Howard & Co., for Cash,				
2 hhds. sugar, 2200 lbs., at 9¢	198	00		
4 " molasses, 252 gals., at 28¢	70	56	268	56
Enter the above entry in the Sales Book and Cash Book.				
4.				
Paid Cash for Rent of Store Room one month	150	00		
Enter on the Credit side of the Cash Book, as entered in the C. B. for this set.				
5.				
Sold B. F. Carpenter, on a/c,				
5 hhds. sugar, 5500 lbs., at 5½¢	302	50		
3 " molasses, 189 gals. at 30¢	56	70	359	20
Enter in the Sales Book, and Journalize the entry in the Journal.				
6.				
Bot. of Chas. Owens,				
50 sacks coffee, 75 lbs, each, at 20¢	750	00		
Paid him cash			375	00
My note at 10 days for			250	00
Bal. on a/c			125	00
Make entries in the Invoice Book, Bill Book, Cash Book, and Journal. As we wish to post the Cash Book to the Ledger, we Debit Chas. Owens in the Cash Book, and Credit him in the Journal for the same amount.				

CHICAGO, APRIL 6, 1872.

Sold W. A. Drew on his note at 10 ds., 11 hhds. sugar, 11000 lbs., at 9¢	990	00		
Make entries in the Journal and Bill Book and Sales Book.				
10.				
I have drawn a draft on B. F. Carpenter at 20 ds. sight, for the balance due me on a/c, which he has accepted this day, for	359	20		
Make entries in the Journal and Bill Book.				
12.				
Sold Hart, Jones & Co., 30 sacks coffee, 2249 lbs., at 25¢	562	25		
Recd. in payment, cash			200	00
Their Note at ten days,			362	25
Enter in the Sales Book, Cash Book and Bill Book, and Journalize the entry. When we Journalize the above entry, we Debit Hart, Jones & Co. in the Journal, for the amount of Cash received, and Debit Cash and Credit Hart, Jones & Co. in the Cash Book for the same amount. The student should bear in mind that when he receives or pays Cash as part payment, he Debits the party he receives Cash from, or Credits the party he pays Cash to, in making the Journal entry, and reverses the same in the Cash Book, that is, Debit in the Cash Book the party credited in the Journal, and Credit in the Cash Book the party debited in the Journal for the same amount. By so doing, the correct balances of the Cash and Personal Accounts are obtained in the Ledger. This is the only practical form if we post the Cash Book to the Ledger. This form is adopted by our best accountants.				
16.				
Recd. of W. A. Drew, cash for his note,				
Face of note	990	00		
Interest on same	2	75	992	75
Enter in the Cash Book on the Debit side, To Bills Rec., Note No. 1, and To Interest, making two entries in the Cash Book.				

CHICAGO, APRIL 17, 1872.

Discounted F. B. Carpenter's acceptance in the City National Bank, at 1% discount.				
Face of draft	359	20		
Discount off			3	59
Recd. cash			355	61
Enter on the Debit side of the Cash Book, To Bills Rec., Note No. 2, and on the Credit side of the Cash Book, By Discount on Bills Rec. No. 2.				
18.				
Bot. of Chapin & Jones, New York,				
25 chests Young Hyson tea, 2000 lbs., at 65¢	1300	00		
50 chests green tea, 4000 lbs., at 75¢	3000	00	4300	00
Paid them my note at 20 ds. for $3500				
Cash 800				
Enter in the Invoice Book, Bill Book, Cash Book, and Journal.				
22.				
Sold Riale Bros., for cash,				
1000 lbs. Young Hyson tea, at 70¢	700	00		
2000 " green tea, " 85"	1700	00	2400	00
Enter in the Sales Book, and on the Dr. side of the Cash Book.				
24.				
Sold Field, Leiter & Co.,				
2000 lbs. green tea, at 85¢	1700	00		
Recd. cash,			1000	00
Their draft on C. Davis, at 10 ds.			500	00
Bal. on a/c			200	00
Enter in the Cash Book, Bill Book, Sales Book, and Journal.				

CHICAGO, APRIL 26, 1872.				
Discounted my note in favor of Chapin & Jones for	3500	00		
At 1% discount.				
Paid cash			3465	00
Discount off			35	00
Enter on the Credit side of the Cash Book, By Bills Pay., Note No. 2; and on the Debit side of the Cash Book, To Discount on Bills Pay., No. 2.	3500	00	35	00
27.				
Sold John Jones, on a/c, 5 hhds. sugar, 5500 lbs., at 9¢	495	00		
Make entries in the Sales Book and Journal.				
29.				
Sold Harvey Day, on a/c, 3 hhds. sugar, 3300 lbs., at 9¢	297	00		
Make entries in the Journal and Sales Book.				
30.				
Sold Riale Brothers, on a/c, 10 hhds. molasses, 630 gals., at 30¢	189	00		
Enter in the Sales Book and Journal.				
Mdse. on hand, as per Inventory,	1101	00		
Required Net Gain or Loss, and Net Capital.				

JOURNAL.

SET 3, NO. 1.

CHICAGO, APRIL 2, 1872.				
Mdse.	2618	75		
To Stewart & Son			2618	75
5.				
B. F. Carpenter	359	20		
To Mdse.			359	20

CHICAGO, APRIL 6, 1872.				
6.				
Mdse..	750	00		
To Bills Pay.			250	00
" Chas Owens			500	00
6.				
Bills Rec.	990	00		
To Mdse.			990	00
10.				
Bills Rec.	359	20		
To B. F. Carpenter			359	20
12.				
Hart, Jones & Co.	200	00		
Bills Rec.	362	25		
To Mdse.			562	25
18.				
Mdse.				
To Chapin & Jones	4300	00		
" Bills Pay.			800	00
			3500	00
24.				
Field, Leiter & Co.	1200	00		
Bills Rec.	500	00		
To Mdse.			1700	00
27.				
John Jones	495	00		
To Mdse.			495	00
29.				
Harvey Day	297	00		
To Mdse.			297	00
30.				
Riale Bros.	189	00		
To Mdse.			189	00

Dr. CASH.

1872.

April	1	To Stock, amount invested in business	√	15,000	00		
"	3	" Mdse., sold Howard & Co.	√	268	56		
"	12	" Hart, Jones & Co., on a/c of Mdse.	√	200	00		
"	16	" Bills Rec. Note No. 1	√	990	00		
"	"	" Interest on " "	√	2	75		
"	17	" Bills Rec. Note No. 2	√	359	20		
"	22	" Mdse., sold Riale Bros.,	√	2,400	00		
"	24	" Field, Leiter & Co., on a/c of Mdse	√	1,000	00		
"	26	" Discount on Bills Pay. No. 2	√	35	00	20,255	51
						20,255	51
May	1	To balance brought down				15,426	92

BILLS.

WHEN REC'D.		No.	IN FAVOR OF	DRAWER OR ACCEPTOR.	DATED.		TIME.
April	6	1	Myself.	W. A. Drew.	April	6	10 Days.
"	10	2	"	B. F. Carpenter.	"	10	20 "
"	12	3	"	Hart, Jones & Co.	"	12	10 "
"	24	4	"	C. B. Davis.	"	24	10 "

BILLS.

WHEN GIVEN.		No.	DRAWER OR ACCEPTOR.	IN FAVOR OF	DATED.		TIME.	PAYABLE AT
April	6	1	Myself.	Chas. Owens.	April	6	10 Days.	1st Nat. Bank
"	18	2	"	Chapin & Jones	"	18	20 "	New York.

CASH. *Cr.*

April	4	By Store Expense, for rent of store	√	150 00	
"	6	" Chas. Owens on a/c of Mdse.	√	375 00	
"	17	" Discount on Bills Rec. No. 2	√	3 59	
"	18	" Chapin & Jones on a/c of Mdse.	√	800 00	
"	26	" Bills Pay. Note No. 2	√	3,500 00	4,828 59
"	30	" *Balance on hand*			15,426 92
					20,255 51

RECEIVABLE.

WHEN DUE.

Year.	Jan.	Feb.	Mar.	Apl.	May	June	July	Aug.	Sept.	Oct.	Nov.	Dec.	Amount.		Remarks.
1872				16									990	00	Received Cash.
"				30									359	20	Rec. Cash less dis't.
"				22									362	25	
"					4								500	00	

PAYABLE.

WHEN DUE.

Year.	Jan.	Feb.	Mar.	Apl.	May	June	July	Aug.	Sept.	Oct.	Nov.	Dec.	Amount.		Remarks.
1872.				16									250	00	
"					8								3500	00	Paid cash less disc't.

Having posted the Journal, the student should post the Cash Book to the Ledger. The Debit of Cash, or the amount, can be posted to the Debit of the Cash Account in the Ledger, making the entry, "To Sunds.," thus debiting cash for the total amount. Then post the credits found on the Dr. of the Cash Book to balance this amount, commencing with Stock, and check each entry in the Cash Book when it is posted. Proceed with the Credit of Cash in the same way. When the same account occurs more than once, the amount can be posted. The Cash Book should be closed when posted, to avoid errors.

The balance of the cash on hand should be brought down on the Dr. of the Cash Account, "To balance brought down," and the amount carried to the second column.

INVOICE BOOK.

The student should have separate books for the Invoice and Sales Books, and enter all Merchandise bought in the Invoice Book, and all Merchandise sold in the Sales Book.

CHICAGO, APRIL 2, 1872.				
Stewart & Son, on a/c, at 10 ds.,				
25 hhds. sugar, 27,500 lbs., at 8¢	2200	00		
1675 gals. molasses, at 25¢	418	75	2618	75
6.				
Chas. Owens, note, cash and on a/c,				
50 sacks coffee, 3750 lbs., at 20¢	750	00		
18.				
Chapin & Jones, note and cash,				
25 chests Young Hyson tea, 2000 lbs., at 65¢	1300	00		
50 chests green tea, 4000 lbs., at 75¢	3000	00	4300	00

SALES BOOK.

CHICAGO, APRIL 3, 1872.				
Howard & Co., for cash,				
2 hhds. sugar, 2200 lbs., at 9¢.	198	00		
4 " molasses, 252 gals. at 28¢	70	56	268	56
5.				
B. F. Carpenter, on a/c,				
5 hhds. sugar, 5500 lbs., at 5½¢	302	50		
3 " molasses, 189 gals., at 30¢	56	70	359	20
6.				
W. A. Drew, on note,				
11 hhds. sugar, 11,000 lbs., at 9¢			990	
12.				
Hart, Jones & Co., for cash and note,				
30 sacks coffee, 2249 lbs., at 25¢			562	25
22.				
Riale Bros., for cash,				
1000 lbs. Young Hyson tea, at 70¢	700	00		
2000 " green tea, at 85¢	1700	00	2400	00
24.				
Field, Leiter & Co., cash, draft and on acct. at 30 ds.,				
2000 lbs. green tea, at 85¢			1700	00
27.				
John Jones, on a/c,				
5 hhds. sugar, 5500 lbs., at 9¢			495	00

Chicago, April 29, 1872.				
Harvey Day, on %c, 3 hhds. sugar, 3300 lbs., at 9¢			297	00
30.				
Riale Bros., on %c, 10 hhds. molasses, 630 gals., at 30¢	189	00		

LEDGER.

No. 1, Set 3.

Dr. Stock. *Cr.*

Apr.	30	*To Bal.*	90	15577	42	Apr.	30	By Cash	82	15000	00
						"	"	" Profit & Loss	90	577	42
				15577	42					15577	42

Dr. Cash. *Cr.*

Apr.	30	To Sunds.	82	20255	51	Apr.	4	By Sunds.	83	4828	59
						"	30	" *Balance*	90	15426	92
										20255	51
May	1	To Balance		15426	92						

No. 1, Set 3.

Dr. MERCHANDISE. *Cr.*

Apr.	2	To Stewart & Sons	80	2618	75	Apr.	5	By B.F.Carpenter	80	359	20
"	6	" Sundries	81	750	00	"	6	" Bills Rec.	81	990	00
"	18	" "	81	4300	00	"	12	" Sundries	81	562	25
"	30	" *Profit & Loss*	90	693	26	"	24	" Sundries	81	1700	00
						"	27	" John Jones	81	495	00
						"	29	" Harvey Day	81	297	00
						"	30	" Riale Bros.	81	189	00
						"	3	" Cash	82	268	56
						"	22	" "	82	2400	00
						"	30	" *Bal. Invt.*	90	1101	00
				8362	01					8362	01
May	1	To Balance Invt.		1101	00						

Dr. STEWART & SONS. *Cr.*

Apr.	30	*To Balance*	90	2618	75	Apr.	2	By Mdse.	80	2618	75
						May	1	By Balance		2618	75

Dr. B. F. CARPENTER. *Cr.*

Apr.	5	To Mdse.	80	359	20	Apr.	10	By Bills Rec.	81	359	20

Dr. BILLS RECEIVABLE. *Cr.*

Apr.	6	To Mdse.	81	990	00	Apr.	16	By Cash	82	990	00
"	10	" B.F.Carpenter	81	359	20	"	17	" "	82	359	20
"	12	" Mdse.	81	362	25	"	30	" *Balance*	90	862	25
"	24	" "	81	500	00						
				2211	45					2211	45
May	1	To Balance		862	25						

Dr. BILLS PAYABLE. *Cr.*

				$	¢					$	¢
Apr.	26	To Cash	83	3500	00	Apr.	6	By Mdse.	81	250	00
Apr.	30	" *Balance*	90	250	00	"	18	" "	81	3500	00
				3750	00					3750	00

Dr. CHAS. OWENS. *Cr*

				$	¢					$	¢
Apr.	6	To Cash	83	375	00	Apr.	6	By Mdse.	81	500	00
"	30	" *Balance*	90	125	00						
				500	00						
						May	1	By Balance		125	00

Dr. HART, JONES & CO. *Cr.*

				$	¢					$	¢
Apr.	12	To Mdse.	81	200	00	Apr.	12	By Cash	82	200	00

Dr. FIELD, LEITER & CO. *Cr.*

				$	¢					$	¢
Apr.	24	To Mdse.	81	1200	00	Apr.	24	By Cash	82	1000	00
						"	30	" *Balance*	90	200	00
"	30	To Bal.		200	00						

Dr. JOHN JONES. *Cr.*

				$	¢					$	¢
Apr.	27	To Mdse.	81	495	00	*Apr.*	30	*By Balance*	90	495	00
May	1	To Balance		495	00						

Dr. HARVEY DAY. *Cr.*

Apr.	29	To Mdse.	81	297	00	*Apr.*	30	*By Balance*	90	297	00
May	1	To Balance		297	00						

Dr. STORE EXPENSE. *Cr.*

Apr,	4	To Cash	83	150	00	*Apr.*	30	*By Profit & Loss*	90	150	00

Dr. RIALE BROTHERS. *Cr.*

Apr.	30	To Mdse.	81	189	00	*Apr.*	30	*By Balance*	90	189	00
May	1	To Balance		189	00						

Dr. CHAPIN & JONES. *Cr.*

Apr.	18	To Cash	83	800	00	Apr.	18	By Mdse.	81	800	00

Dr. DISCOUNT. *Cr.*

Apr.	17	To Cash	83	3	59	Apr.	26	By Cash	82	35	00
"	30	" *Profit & Loss*	90	31	41						
				35	00					35	00

Dr. INTEREST. *Cr.*

Apr.	30	*To Profit & Loss*	90	2	75	Apr.	16	By Cash	82	2	75

Dr. PROFIT AND LOSS. *Cr.*

Apr.	30	To Store Expense	89	150	00	Apr.	30	By Mdse.	87	693	26
"	"	" *Stock*	86	577	42		"	" Discount	89	31	41
							"	" Interest	89	2	75
				727	42					727	42

Dr. BALANCE. *Cr.*

Apr.	30	To Mdse. Invt.	87	1101	00	Apr.	30	By Stewart & Sons	87	2618	75
"	"	" Cash	86	15426	92	"	"	" Bills Pay	88	250	00
"	"	" Bills Rec.	87	862	25	"	"	" Chas. Owens	88	125	00
"	"	" Field, Leiter & Co.	88	200	00	"	"	" *Stock*	86	15577	42
"	"	" John Jones	88	495	00						
"	"	" Harvey Day	89	297	00						
"	"	" Riale Bros.	89	189	00						
				18571	17					18571	17

STUDENT.

May 1	By Net Capital	15577	42

SET 4, NO. 1.

The student is supposed to continue in business, in this set, with the Resources and Liabilities in the Balance Account for Set 3, but admits John Smith as a partner, with a cash capital equal to the Student's Net Capital, amounting to $15,577.42.

As the Debit of Balance exhibits a list of the Resources, and the Credit a list of the Liabilities, you can open your books by making the entry in the Journal, "Sunds. to Stock," giving Stock credit for the total amount, and debit each item found in the list of the Resources.

HOW TO RE-OPEN A SET OF BOOKS.

The most practical method to re-open a Set of Books, is to bring down the Balances, showing Resources and Liabilities, either under the old accounts where there is room, or open new accounts where more space is needed.

In the Balance Account on page 90, is found a list of the Resources and Liabilities on closing the Books the last of April.

The Net Capital as shown in the Stock Balance on the Credit of the Balance Account, is $15,577.42. The Student is now to form a Copartnership with John Smith, who is to invest a Cash Capital equal to the Net Capital of the Student, which is shown above to be $15,577.42, and to share equally in Gains and Losses during the following month of May. The name of the new firm is now the Student's name and Smith. First bring down the Cash Balance found in the Cash Book, page 83, to the Debit side of the Cash Book, and make the entry in black ink, May 1, to Balance $15,426,92, writing the figures in the first column.

Next make the entry on the Debit side of the Cash Book to John Smith, $15,577.42. Next open an account in the Ledger with the Student, also separate accounts with John Smith, Mdse., Bills Rec., Field, Leiter & Co., John Jones, Harvey Day, Riale Bros., Stewart & Sons, Bills Pay. and Chas. Owens. Debit each of the accounts found on the Debit of Balance on page 90, to Balance for the amount of the Balance given in the Balance Account. Hereafter open no account with Cash in the Ledger, but bring the Cash Balance down in the Cash Book whenever the Cash Book is closed and re-opened. The Student should understand that the Cash Book constitutes the same thing as a Cash Account in the Ledger when posted.

The new accounts opened in the Ledger which are transferred from the Credit of the Balance Account, should be Credited by Balance for the amount of each of the Balances shown in the Balance account on page 90.

As no Stock Account is kept in Partnership, transfer the Stock Balance to the Credit of the Student's account. Close the Cash Book and bring the Cash Balance on the Debit of the Cash Account when a First Trial Balance is taken, also carry the same Balance to the Debit of the Balance Account when the Ledger is closed.

The Student should now write up a Journal, and Cash Book, Sales, Invoice and Bill Books for the month of May, using the same forms, and follow the same rules as given for Wholesaling in April.

MEMORANDA OF BUSINESS.

Set 4, No. 1.

Chicago, May 2, 1873.				
Bot. of Austin & Gibbs, N. Y., on a/c,				
100 boxes raisins, at $3	300	00		
500 " oranges, at $2.75	1375	00	1675	00
3.				
Bot. of Robt. Haywood, at 10 ds.,				
10 hhds. sugar, 11,000 lbs., at 9¢	990	00		
10 sacks coffee, 750 lbs., at 20¢	150	00	1140	00
4.				
Sold Geo. Whitney, on a/c at 10 ds.,				
50 boxes raisins, at $3.50	175	00		
100 " oranges, at $3.25	325	00	500	00
In business, goods are usually sold on 30, 60 or 90 days. We have made the time 10 days, because we could arrange the entries more satisfactorily.				
5.				
Bot. of R. C. Spencer, on our note at 10 ds.,				
500 boxes lemons, at $3	1500	00		
10 hhds. sugar, 11,000 lbs., at 8¢	880	00	2380	00
6.				
Accepted Austin & Gibbs' draft on us at 2 ds. for	1675	00		
8.				
Paid cash to Robt. Haywood on a/c	990	00		

Chicago, May 9, 1872.

Paid cash for our acceptance, Austin & Gibbs' favor	1675	00		
"				
Shipped to Geo. Hoffman, Buffalo, N. Y., to be sold on joint a/c each ½,				
200 boxes oranges, at $2.75 $550				
5 hhds. sugar, 5500 lbs., at 8¢ 440				
100 boxes lemons, at $3 300	1290	00		
Geo. Hoffman's ½ invoice is			645	00
Shipt. to Buffalo, Co. A			645	00
Enter in the Journal, Sunds. to Mdse., and give Mdse. credit for the full amount of the shipment	1290	00		
Debit Geo. Hoffman for half of the invoice, $645, as he buys half interest on acct.				
Debit shipt. to Buffalo, Co. A, for the amount of your half shipt., $645.				
"				
Sold L. Friend,				
5 sacks coffee, 375 lbs., at 22¢	82	50		
10 hhds. sugar, 1100 lbs., at 9¢	990	00	1072	50
Recd. in paymt.,				
Sight draft on N. French for $500				
Cash 400				
Bal. on a/c 172.50				
"				
Bot. of Durand & Co.,				
10 hhds. molasses, 640 gals., at 80¢	512	00		
20 bbls. A sugar, 5700 lbs., at 9½¢	541	50		
10 chests Y. H. tea, 450 lbs., at $1	450	00		
10 bags Rio coffee, 840 lbs., at 20¢	168	00	1671	50
Paid our note at 10 ds. for $1,000.00				
Cash for bal. 671.50				
13.				
Paid cash for rent of Store	150	00		
Gas bill for Store	20	00	170	00

CHICAGO, MAY 14, 1872.

Geo. Whitney having become insolvent, we have accepted 25% of the amount he owes us, on a/c, and lose the balance.				
Recd. cash	125	00		
Lose	375	00	500	00
The above entry should be made in the Cash Book on the Debit side To Geo. Whitney, for	500	00		
And on the Credit side, By Profit and Loss on Geo. Whitney's acct., $375.00.				
15.				
The Student drew cash from the firm for private use	125	00		
"				
John Smith drew cash for private use, amounting to	150	00		
" .				
Sold J. W. Jackson, on a/c,				
200 boxes lemon, at $3.50	700	00		
5 bags coffee, 400 lbs., at 23¢	92	00	792	00
17.				
Sold Joseph Friedman,				
8 hhds. molasses, 510 gals., at 90¢	459	00		
100 boxes lemons, at $3.50	350	00		
50 " oranges, " 3.00	150	00	959	00
Recd. cash $400				
Geo. Davis' note at 10 ds. 380				
Bal. on a/c 179	959	00		
19.				
Paid cash for safe for Store	500	00		
Credit Cash in Cash Book, and debit Store Fixtures.				

Chicago, May 20, 1872.				
Bot. of Wm. Lyman, 2000 bbls. salt, at $3 Paid cash Bal. on a/c	6000	00	4000 2000	00 00
21.				
Sold H. M. Newell, on note at 8 ds., 10 chests Young Hyson tea, 450 lbs., at $1.10 500 bbls. salt, at $3.25	495 1625	00 00	2120	00
22.				
The thieves broke into our Store last night, and carried off Mdse. valued at	600	00		
"				
Sold S. J. Kline, for cash, 1000 bbls. salt, at $3.10	3100	00		
23.				
Paid Emanuel Friedman cash for services in the store	50	00		
24.				
The thieves that broke open our Store have been arrested, and Mdse. recovered amounting to	500	00		
"				
Paid Detective Simons, for arresting the thieves and recovery of goods, a reward of	150	00		

CHICAGO, MAY 25, 1872.				
Bot. of J. W. Doane & Co., 100 bags Java coffee, 8500 lbs., at 21¢	1785	00		
200 boxes raisins, at $2.75	550	00	2335	00
Paid them cash $1000				
Our draft on J. W. Jackson 700				
Our note for 30 ds. 300				
Bal. on a/c 335	2335	00		
"				
The Student drew cash from the firm for private use	125	00		
John Smith drew cash from the firm amounting to	150	00		
27.				
Shipped to C. W. Downs & Co., New York, to be sold on our acct. and risk,				
200 boxes raisins, at $3	600	00		
60 bags coffee, 5000 lbs., at 21¢	1050	00		
50 boxes oranges, at $2.75	137	50	1787	50
Paid cash for drayage			12	50
Debit Shipt. to N. Y. for $1800.				
"				
Recd. cash of L. Friend in full on a/c	172	50		
28.				
Paid Durand & Co., cash for our note, No. ——, in their favor, for	1000	00		
Interest on the same for 20 ds. at 10% per annum	5	56	1005	56
"				
Paid Wm. Lyman cash on a/c	1000	00		

CHICAGO, MAY 28, 1872.

Bot. of D. Cole & Sons,				
House and lot, No. 441 W. Washington Street, Chicago, for	20000	00		
Paid them cash			8000	00
Bal. in notes at 1, 2 and 3 years, at 8% per annum, for			12000	00
29.				
Recd. cash of H. M. Newell, for his note, our favor, for	2120	00		
Interest on same for 8 ds. at 10% per annum	4	71	2124	71
"				
Recd. cash of Geo. Hoffman, on a/c	645	00		
" for net proceeds of		00		
Shipt. to Buffalo Co. A. cash.	750	00	1395	00
30.				
Sold A. P. Andrews,				
10 bbls. A sugar, 2850 lbs., at 10¢	285	00		
2 hhds. molasses, 130 gals., at $1	130	00		
100 boxes lemons, at $3.50	350	00		
500 bbls. salt, at $3.25	1625	00	2390	00
Recd. in paymt., our note, R. C. Spencer's favor $2380				
Cash for balance 10	2390	00		
31.				
Paid H. Barbier cash for repairs on house on Washington Street	250	00		
Debit Real Estate.				
Property on hand:				
Mdse. as per inventory	3246	25		
Real Estate	20250	00		
Shipt. to N. Y.	1800	00		
Store fixtures	500	00		

THE STUDENT AND JOHN SMITH'S BALANCE SHEET FOR MAY.

	L. Fol.	Ledger Bals. Dr.		Ledger Bals. Cr.		Prop'ty Unsold.		Profit & Loss Dr.		Profit & Loss Cr.		Student. Dr.		Student. Cr.		John Smith. Dr.		John Smith. Cr.		Balance. Res'rces		Balance. Liab'ties	
Student				15327	42									15327	42								
John Smith				15277	42													15277	42				
Cash		18706	99																	18706	99		
Mdse.		2191	50			3246	25			1054	75									3246	25		
Stewart & Sons				2618	75																	2618	75
Bills Receivable		1742	25																	1742	25		
Bills Payable				12550	00																	12550	00
Chas Owens				125	00																	125	00
Field, Leiter & Co.		200	00																	200	00		
John Jones		495	00																	495	00		
Harvey Day		297	00																	297	00		
Riale Bros		189	00																	189	00		
Robert Haywood				150	00																	150	00
Ship. to Buffalo, Co. A				105	00					105	00												
Store Expense		370	00					370	00														
Store Fixtures		500	00			500	00													500	00		
J. W. Jackson		92	00																	92	00		
Jos. Friedman		179	00																	179	00		
Wm. Lyman				1000	00																	1000	00
J. W. Doane & Co.				335	00																	335	00
Shipped to N. Y., Co. A.		1800	00			1800	00													1800	00		
Interest			85						85														
Real Estate		20250	00			20250	00													20250	00		
Profit and Loss		475	00					475	00														
		47488	59	47488	59	25796	25																
To Student for one-half Net Gain,								156	95					156	95								
To John Smith for one-half Net Gain,								156	95									156	95				
								1159	75	1159	75												
To balance for Student's Net Capital,												15484	37									15484	37
" " " John Smith's Net Capital,																15434	37					15434	37
												15484	37	15484	37	15434	37	15434	37	47697	49	47697	49

FORMS FOR RETAILING.

SET 5. NO. 1.

This set teaches the practical forms for retailing, and will be found convenient for many branches of business.

No Day Book is kept. Where goods are bought or sold for cash, the entry is made in the Cash Book. If they are bought or sold on account, the history is given in the Journal.

Keep a Journal, Bill Book, Cash Book, and Ledger. A petty Cash Book is sometimes kept, which is really a memoranda of the cash received and paid out, which should be transferred to the general Cash Book. Sometimes the business requires a number of auxiliary books, depending upon the nature and kind of business. A Letter Book is used, if you wish to preserve a copy of your letters. An Order Book is frequently kept as a memorandum for purchases. A blank Pass Book, and a Check Book should be kept if you make deposits in the bank.

It will be necessary for the accountant to exercise good judgment in selecting the forms, and the kind of books his business requires. Accountants vary in selecting the forms, and the manner of keeping the accounts, yet the same results should be obtained, and will be, if the books are correctly kept.

The most convenient method of keeping the Mdse. Account is to enter each day on the debit of the Cash Book, "To Mdse. Sales," for the day, for the total amount of cash received for Mdse. on the day the entry is made.

If Cash is received or paid on account, the entry should be made in the Cash Book. Every entry made in the Cash Book should be Journalized when the entry is made, as the Cash Book is not only used to keep an account with Cash, but it is used to express Journal entries, and a history of the cash transactions, and can be posted directly from this book to the Ledger, not forgetting to check in the Cash Book every entry posted.

This book should not be posted until it is closed, but the accountant should find the balance of the Cash Book every day, which should agree with the amount on hand. This can be done by footing the debit and credit of the Cash Account, on waste paper If the Cash Book is closed, bring the balance to the debit side, in the second column, using the first column for cash received, and carry the amount to the second column when it is closed or footed. Observe the same rule on the credit side.

MEMORANDA.

SET 5. NO. 1.

CHICAGO, JUNE 1, 1872.				
Commenced business with a cash capital of	5000	00		
The above entry should be made on the debit of the C. B., "To Stock," amount invested.				
2.				
Bot. of J. V. Farwell & Co.,				
Mdse. as per invoice	2700	00		
Paid cash			1500	00
Balance on a/c			1200	00
Make the Journal entry "Mdse. To J. V. Farwell & Co.," for the full amount, and credit cash for the amount paid, in the C. B., "By J. V. Farwell & Co., on a/c of Mdse."				
3.				
Sold for cash Mdse. amounting to	250	00		
Debit cash in the C. B., "To Mdse." sales for the day.				
4.				
Sold F. M. Munson on a/c,				
15 yds. French poplin at 75¢	11	25		
22 " black silk at $2	44	00		
25 " sheeting at 15¢	3	75	59	00
Make the following entry in the Journal:				
F. M. Munson,	59	00		
To Mdse. sold on a/c,			59	00
15 yds. French poplin at 75c, $11.25				
22 " black silk at $2, 44.00				
25 " sheeting at 15c, 3.75 $59.				

CHICAGO, JUNE 5, 1872.				
Sold Geo. Loring for his note at 30 ds. a bill of Mdse. amounting to	125	00		
Make entries in the Bill Book and Journal.				
6.				
Received cash for Mdse. sold this day amounting to	375	00		
8.				
Paid cash for rent of store room	50	00		
"				
Received cash for Mdse.	250	00		
9.				
Sold W. Wright on a/c,				
7 yds. broadcloth at $2.50	17	50		
1 silk hat	6	00		
1 neck tie		75	24	25
10.				
Received cash of F. M. Munson on a/c	25	00		
Debit Cash in the C. B., and credit F. M. Munson.				
"				
Bot. a bill of Mdse. of Hamlin, Hale & Co.,	1200	00		
Paid my note at ten days for			1200	00
Make entries in the Journal and B. B.				
11.				
Paid cash for groceries	10	65		

CHICAGO, JUNE 12, 1872.				
Paid J. V. Farwell & Co. cash on a/c	500	00		
"				
Received cash for Mdse.	230	00		
13.				
Paid cash to Daniel Roberts for services in the store	25	00		
"				
Sold Robert Morris, on a/c,				
3 pairs gents' boots, at $5	15	00		
12 pairs gents' cotton socks, at 35¢	4	20		
15 yds. black ribbon, at 50¢	7	50	26	70
15.				
Sold Wm. Baxter on a/c				
50 yds. sheeting, at 15¢	7	50		
25 yds prints, at 12½¢	3	13	10	63
16.				
Robt. Jones has discounted his note for			125	00
Recd. cash	120	00		
Discount on his note	5	00		
Debit Cash in the C. B. "To Bills Rec.,"	125	00		
and credit Cash "By Discount,"			5	00
18.				
Recd. cash for Mdse.,	175	00		
19.				
Paid J. V. Farwell & Co. cash on a/c	350	00		

CHICAGO, JUNE 20, 1872.				
Received cash of Wm. Baxter on a/c	5	00		
22.				
Robert Morris paid me on a/c with Gilbert Harris' note, made June 1, due July 1,	20	00		
Make entries in Journal and B. B.				
"				
Sold Geo. Richardson, on a/c,				
27 yds. French poplin, at 75¢	20	25		
45 " black silk, at $2	90	00		
100 yds. sheeting, at 15¢	15	00	125	25
"				
Bot. of Field, Leiter & Co.,				
Mdse. as per invoice	750	00		
Paid cash			300	00
My note at six days			450	00
"				
Paid cash for my note and interest Hamlin, Hale & Co.'s favor,				
Face of note	1200	00		
Interest	2	00	1202	00
Credit Cash " By Bills Pay."	1200	00		
" " By Interest	2	00		
23.				
Sold Wm. Watson, on a/c,				
5 yds. Irish linen, at 75¢	3	75		
12 yds. black cambric, at 20¢	2	40	6	15

CHICAGO, JUNE 23, 1872.				
Paid J. V. Farwell & Co., on a/c, with my draft on Geo. Richardson	75	00		
Journalize the entry.				
24.				
Bot. of Robert Morris, on a/c, 25 lbs. butter for family use, at 20¢	5	00		
Debit "Family Expense," to Robert Morris.				
25.				
Paid Field, Leiter & Co., cash on a/c	250	00		
Paid J. V. Farwell & Co., cash on a/c	175	00		
26.				
Received cash for Mdse.	175	25		
28.				
Paid Field, Leiter & Co.,				
Cash for my note	450	00		
Interest		75	450	75
"				
Sold John Williams for cash, a bill of Mdse. amounting to	75	75		
Debit Cash "To Mdse. sold John Williams."				
Mdse. on hand, as per inventory	3225	00		
Post the Journal to the Ledger, then close and post the Cash Book. Required, the net gain or loss.				

MEMORANDA FOR JULY.

J. T. Wheeler and M. R. Brown have this day formed a copartnership in a Retail Gents' Furnishing Establishment. They are to invest equal amounts, and share equally in the gains and losses.

CHICAGO, JULY 1, 1872.				
J. T. Wheeler invested cash	2500	00		
Mdse., as per inventory	1000	00		
Bills Rec., as per B. B.	500	00	4000	00
M. R. Brown invested cash	2000	00		
Bills Rec.	700	00		
Geo. C. Oakley owes him on a/c	300	00		
Mdse as per inventory	1000	00	4000	00
J. T. Wheeler owes J. Lacy on his note, which is assumed by the firm,	500	00		
M. R. Brown owes H. Lewis on a/c	250	00		
Henry Dwight on a/c	250	00	500	00
2.				
Sold David Fuller, on a/c,				
1 pair doeskin pants	9	00		
2 boxes Gray's collars		70	9	70
3.				
Sold Mdse., for cash	75	00		
4.				
Sold J. Lacy, on a/c,				
1 overcoat	30	00		
1 vest	9	00	39	00
5.				
Paid J. Lacy cash for J. T. Wheeler's note	500	00		
Interest on the same	5	00		

CHICAGO, JULY 6, 1872.				
Recd. cash for Mdse. sales	180	00		
8.				
Recd. cash for D. Merrill's note	250	00		
Interest on the note	25	00	275	00
9.				
Bot. of Weber & Harkin, on a/c,				
Mdse. as per invoice	725	75		
10.				
Paid H. Lewis on a/c, with our draft on Geo. C. Oakley	250	00		
11.				
Sold John Dunham, on a/c,				
1 wedding suit, per contract	65	00		
12.				
Recd. cash of H. Dwight, on a/c	75	00		
13.				
Paid cash for 4 tons coal for use of the store	40	00		
15.				
Sold J. M. Stevens, on a/c,				
1 neck tie	1	25		
5 boxes cuffs, at 25¢	1	25		
1 pair sleeve buttons		75	3	25
16.				
Recd. cash of David Fuller, on a/c	5	00		

CHICAGO, JULY 17, 1872.				
Sold Mdse. for cash	180	00		
18.				
J. T. Wheeler drew cash	75	00		
M. R. Brown " "	75	00	150	00
19.				
Sold Wm. E. Bowman, for cash,				
1 frock coat	25	00		
1 vest	8	00		
1 pair pants	10	00	43	00
20.				
Recd. cash of J. M. Stevens, on a/c,	3	25		
22.				
Paid Weber & Harkin cash on a/c	250	00		
23.				
Sold J. W. Raymond, on a/c,				
5 pairs cotton hose, at 25¢	1	25		
2 linen handkerchiefs, at 40¢		80		
1 box Gray's collars		35		
1 " cuffs		40	2	80
24.				
Sold Colby Drew, on a/c,				
1 wedding suit, as per contract	125	00		
25.				
Sold James Reed, on a/c,				
1 velvet coat	45	00		
1 silk neck tie	2	50	47	50

Chicago, July 26, 1872.				
Colby Drew paid us on a/c with his draft on the City National Bank	125	00		
28.				
Paid cash for rent of store, 1 month	75	00		
30.				
Recd. cash for Mdse.	250	00		
Mdse. on hand, as per inventory	1720	00		
Required net gain or loss, and net capital of each partner.				

MEMORANDA FOR RETAILING.

Inventory of the joint resources of A. Spicer and F. P. Stone, who have this day entered into partnership under the firm title of Spicer & Stone, each to share one-half of the gains or losses.

Chicago, August 1, 1872.				
A. Spicer invested cash	2500	00		
F. P. Stone invested cash	2500	00		
Paid cash as follows:				
For rent of store	75	00		
" printing cards and bill heads	8	00	83	00
shelvings, safe, counters, etc.	395	00	395	00
2.				
Bot. of Hamlin, Hale & Co.,				
A bill of Mdse. amounting to	1800	00		
Paid them cash			750	00
Our note at 30 ds. for			600	00
Bal. on a/c			450	00

Chicago, August 3, 1872.				
Bot. of Field, Leiter & Co.,				
A bill of Mdse. amounting to	1146	00		
Paid our note at 30 ds. for			1146	00
5.				
Recd. cash for Mdse. sold this day	38	00		
6.				
Sold L. McAndrews on a/c,				
20 yds. of sheeting, at 11¢	2	20		
10 " Irish poplin, " 80¢	8	00	10	20
"				
Paid cash for repairing lock at store	1	80		
7.				
Sold Mrs. R. Watson,				
48 yds. sheeting, at 10¢	4	80		
3 table cloths, " $1.25	3	75		
15 yds. alpaca, " 60¢	9	00	17	55
Recd. cash 12.00				
Bal. on a/c 5.55				
"				
Recd. cash for Mdse. sales	45	00		
9.				
Sold S. Brown on a/c,				
1 lace shawl	60	00		
"				
Recd. cash of Mrs. Watson on a/c	4	00		

Chicago, August 10, 1872.				
Bot. of Gage, Mallory & Co.,				
A bill of Mdse. amounting to	198	00		
Paid our note at 30 ds. amounting to			100	00
Cash for balance			98	00
"				
Sold S. Jones on a/c,				
1 doz. spools of thread		72		
1 " papers pins		60		
11 yds. black lace, at 80¢	8	80	10	12
11.				
Recd. of L. McAndrews on a/c, his order on R. Johnson for	10	20		
"				
Recd. cash for sales of Mdse.	85	00		
12.				
Sold A. Buckminster,				
16 yds. silk, at $3.50	56	00		
Recd. his sight draft on Hamlin, Hale & Co. for			50	00
Cash for bal.			6	00
"				
A. Spicer drew cash for personal use	30	00		
F. P. Stone " " " "	35	00		
14.				
Recd. cash for sales of Mdse.	100	00		
"				
Paid cash for painting front of store	38	00		

CHICAGO, AUGUST 15, 1872.

Sold B. R. Styles,				
56 yds. muslin, at 10¢	5	60		
1 doz. hair nets	2	50	8	10
Recd. cash $4.00				
Bal. on a/c 4.10				
"				
Paid cash as follows:				
For pens and ink $1.40				
" window brush 2.00				
" one pane glass 3.40	6	80		
16.				
Recd. cash for sales of Mdse.	89	00		
17.				
Bot. of Sweet, Dempster & Co.,				
Mdse. amounting to	395	00		
Paid cash			295	00
Our note at 30 ds. for			100	00
"				
Sold Wm. Goodrich on a/c,				
20 yds. black alpaca, at $1.00	20	00		
10 " " lace, " 1.25	12	50	32	50
18.				
A. Spicer drew cash for personal use	40	00		
F. P. Stone " " " "	40	00		
"				
Bot. of Sam'l J. Kline on a/c,				
A bill of Mdse. amounting to	381	00		

CHICAGO, AUGUST 18, 1872.				
Recd. cash for sales of Mdse.	107	00		
20.				
Sold Chas. V. Smith, 15 yds. cambric, at 15¢ 18 " linen, " 18½ 2 india rubber combs, " 40 Recd. cash $2.00 Bal. on a/c 4.38	2 3	25 33 80	6	38
21.				
Recd. of W. Goodrich, cash on a/c	25	00		
"				
Recd. cash for sales of Mdse.	121	00		
22.				
Paid cash for scrubbing floor	2	00		
23.				
Sold C. C. Collins on a/c, 30 yds. black braid, at 10¢ 12 " Scotch plaid, " 50	3 6	00 00	9	00
"				
Sold W. Barber on a/c, 1 piece muslin, 40 yds., at 10¢ 3 window shades, at $1.00	4 3	00 00	7	00
24.				
Paid S. J. Kline, cash on a/c	100	00		

CHICAGO, AUGUST 24, 1872.				
Recd. cash for sales of Mdse.	110	00		
"				
Sold J. R. Deaton,				
28 yds. calico, at 10¢	2	80		
30 " delaine, " 12	3	60	6	40
Recd. cash			2	50
Bal. on a/c			3	90
25.				
Bot. of Hamlin, Hale & Co., for cash,				
Mdse. amounting to	218	00		
"				
Paid cash for whitewashing store	8	00		
26.				
Sold Bernard Montague,				
22 yds. black alpaca, at 50¢	11	00		
Recd. cash $5.00				
Bal. on a/c 6.00				
27.				
Recd. cash for sales of Mdse.	119	00		
28.				
Sold S. M. Matson, on a/c,				
30 yds. musquito bar, at 30¢	9	00		
"				
Paid S. J. Kline, cash on a/c	50	00		

CHICAGO, AUGUST 29, 1872.				
Bot. of E. F. Hollister & Co., on a/c, 50 yds. oil cloth, at 60¢	30	00		
"				
Recd. cash for sales of Mdse.	78	00		
30.				
Sold E. P. Saddler, on a/c, 20 yds. black alpaca, at $1.00	20	00		
"				
Paid E. F. Hollister & Co., cash on a/c	20	00		
31.				
Paid Hamlin, Hale & Co.,				
Cash for our note	600	00		
Interest on the same	5	00	605	00
Mdse. on hand, as per inventory	3250	00		
Store Fixtures	395	00		
Post, close, and make out a Balance Sheet.				

TO CHANGE BOOKS FROM SINGLE TO DOUBLE ENTRY.

Close your books, take an inventory, and make a statement in your Journal, by making the entry "Sunds. to Stock." Debit the items that make up a list of your resources, and Credit Stock for the full amount. Debit Stock for the amount of your Liabilities, and credit the items that make up this list.

COMMISSION.

The forms for Commission vary in different kinds of business. This form given for Produce Commission has been adopted by a majority of the business houses in the Produce Commission business in Chicago.

Whenever a consignment is received, it is numbered from one to higher numbers inclusively in the Commission Sales Book, and a corresponding number placed on all packages received at the same time, from the same consigner. A Cash Book is kept, and cash paid for charges on freight and cartage is entered in this book, giving cash credit and debiting mdse. Whenever a sale is made from any of these consignments, mdse. should be credited. When a consignment is all sold, an account sales should be made and sent to the consigner; and if cash is remitted to the shipper, credit cash and debit mdse. for the net proceeds. If only an account sales is sent, debit mdse. and credit the party who shipped the goods for the net proceeds. By this method it is not necessary to open an account with the shipper, if the net proceeds are sent with the account sales when the goods are all sold.

When a sale is made from any of the consignments, enter the same in the voucher, as shown in the Commission Sales Book, also the charges; and when the goods are all sold, compute the commission and subtract the total charges from the gross sales, and bring down the net proceeds and copy from the voucher to the account sales, which, in actual business, is sent to the shipper. Sometimes the salesman keeps a Receiving and Sales Book with a pencil, and the book-keeper copies the same.

In this work keep only Commission Sales Book, Cash Book, Journal, and post to Ledger.

PRODUCE COMMISSION.

Wm. Lyman, Samuel Sargent, and Amos Brown have this day formed a copartnership, under the firm name of Lyman, Sargent & Co. Each partner invests $5000 in cash for the purpose of engaging in the Produce and Commission business. Dr. cash in C. B., and Cr. each partner for the amt. invested

	CHICAGO, SEPT. 1, 1881.		
	Bot. of Sprague, Warner & Co., for cash,		
	150 bbls. flour, at $8.75		
	2.		
No. 1.	Recd. from Bennett & Riale, Ottawa, Ill., to be sold on their ᵃ/c and risk,		
	10 tubs butter, 75 lbs. each		
	Gross, tare, 5½ lbs. each		
	Enter in the C. S. B., as shown for No. 1 Voucher.		
	3.		
	Paid cash for freight on Bennett & Riale's con.		
	Freight	4	50
	Drayage		50
	Enter in Cash Book and on Voucher of Com. Sales Book.		
	"		
No. 2.	Recd. from Stewart Bros., Elgin, Ill., to be sold on their ᵃ/c and risk,		
	500 bu. potatoes		
	Paid cash for freight	12	75
	" " " drayage	5	20
	Enter in C. S. B. for No. 2, also in Cash Book.		
	5.		
	Sold John King & Sons, for cash,		
	Con. No. 1, 5 tubs butter 75—5½ at 18¢		
	Compute sale on 69½ lbs., net weight, for each tub. Dr. cash and Cr. mdse. in Cash Book.		
	6.		
	Sold A. B. Harvey, on ᵃ/c,		
	50 bbls. flour, at $9.55		
	Paid cash for rent of store	75	00
	" " book-keeper	25	00

CHICAGO, SEPT. 8, 1881.		
Sold Stewart Bros. con. for cash, 300 bu. potatoes, at 95¢ Bennett & Riale's con., 5 tubs butter 75—5½, at 20¢ Make entries in Vouchers Nos. 1 and 2, and Cash Book.		
"		
Made out a/c sales to Bennett & Riale for net proceeds, and remitted cash for the same. Commission computed at 5% on these consignments Make an a/c sales. Cr. cash and Dr. mdse.		
9.		
Sold Wm. Hinman, on his note, 25 bbls. flour, at $9.87½		
"		
Sold Peter Cooper, on a/c Stewart & Bros. con. No. 2, 200 bu potatoes, at 87¢		
10.		
Closed Stewart Bros. con., and remitted only the a/c sales. Dr. mdse. and Cr. Stewart Bros. for net proceeds.		
"		
Recd. cash of A. B. Harvey, on a/c	250	00

CHICAGO, SEPT. 11, 1881.

No. 3.	Recd. from A. S. Kimball, So. Royalton, Vt., to be sold on his a/c and risk,		
	4600 lbs. maple sugar		
	50 cases eggs		
	75 bbls. apples		
	Paid cash for freight	15	00
	" " " drayage	1	50
	12.		
	Sold Thos. Wood, con. No. 3, for cash,		
	2000 lbs. maple sugar, at 9¢		
	"		
No. 4.	Recd. from Chas. Abbott & Co, St. Joseph, Mich., to be sold on their a/c and risk,		
	50 baskets peaches		
	60 cases eggs		
	150 cases blueberries		
	13.		
	Paid cash for freight,		
	Abbott & Co.'s consignment	3	50
	Drayage		75
	15.		
	Sold Chas. Abbott & Co.'s con. for cash,		
	50 baskets peaches, at 56¢		
	20 cases eggs, at $18		
	50 " blueberries, at 75¢		
	16.		
	Sold the balance of No. 3 con. for cash,		
	Sugar, at 9¾¢		
	Eggs, at $20 per case		
	Apples, at $3 per bbl.		

CHICAGO, SEPT. 17, 1881.

Sold Otto Formhals, on a/c con. No. 4,
50 cases blueberries, at $1.25,

18.

Sold Chas. Morey, for cash, No. 4,
50 cases blueberries, at $1.20
40 " eggs, at $19.50

19.

Rendered a/c sales to No. 3 con., and remitted a sight draft on First National Bank, for which we paid cash,
Paid cash for exchange | | 50

Cr. cash and Dr. mdse. for net proceeds, and Dr. expense for the exchange.

20.

Make a/c sales for No. 4, and remit cash for net proceeds.

"

Paid Chas. Curtis, cash for 2 weeks' salary as book-keeper | 50 | 00

22.

No. 5. Recd. from G. S. Butler, Ottawa, Ill., to be sold on his a/c and risk,
1200 lbs. cheese
20 tubs butter, 65—4¾ lbs.

23.

Recd. cash of Otto Formhals, on a/c | 20 | 20

Chicago, Sept. 23, 1881.		
Paid cash for con. No. 5,		
Freight	25	75
Drayage	2	75
24.		
Sold Wm. Trabing, on a/c, con. No. 5,		
500 lbs. cheese, at 13¢		
"		
Sold M. M. McNair, con. No. 5,		
700 lbs. cheese, at 13½¢		
Recd. in payment, cash	50	00
His draft on A. B. Harvey	20	00
Stewart Bros'. draft on us	15	00
Balance on a/c		
"		
Sold M. E. Drew, on a/c con. No. 5,		
12 tubs butter, 65 lbs. gross, 4¾ tare, at 15¢ net weight		
25.		
Sold Chas. Warner, on a/c,		
Balance of con. No. 5, at 16¼¢ per lb., net weight		
26.		
Recd. cash of W. Trabing, on a/c	32	23
" " " M. E. Drew, " "	52	50
" " " Chas. Warner, on a/c	18	00
"		
Sold E. J. Colwell, for cash,		
30 bbls. flour, at $10.20		

CHICAGO, SEPT. 26, 1881.

Closed con. No. 5, and remitted the a/c sales only

27.

Find am't. of mdse. on hand, and take an inventory

Post, close, and make balance sheet.

INVOICES.

No. 1.

CHICAGO, Sept. 12, 1882.

GEO. DAVIS.

Bot. of H. O. WILLIAMS.

135 lbs. Rio Coffee at 27¢
132 " W I. Sugar at 8½¢
127 " Pearl Starch at 13½¢
142 " Butter Crackers at 12½¢
37 " Soda Crackers at 13¢
143 " Granulated Sugar at 8½¢
46 " Butter at 17¾¢

Paid. H. O. WILLIAMS.

No. 2.

CHICAGO, Sept. 12, 1882.

CHAS. DOWNS.

Bot. of R. J. HOWE.

19 yds. Blk. Silk at 95¢
18 " Ribbon at 42¢
165 yds. Muslin at 15¼¢
13 yds. Cassimere at $1.52
12½ yds. Broadcloth at $3.25
17 yds. Doeskin at $1.12½
1 Cravat, $1.25
3 pairs Boots at $4.35
1½ doz. Sleeve Buttons at 62¢
3½ " Collars at $2.30
2 doz. Handkerchiefs at $1.35
5 doz. Gents' Socks at $1.55

Paid. R. J. HOWE.

VOUCHER.

No. 1. SEPT. 2, 1881.

Of 10 tubs butter, 75 lbs.—5½ each.

For BENNETT & RIALE,

Residence, OTTAWA, ILL.

1881.					
Sept. 5	5 tubs, 69½, 347½ lbs., at 18c	62	55		
" 8	5 tubs, 347½, at 20c	69	50	132	05
	Freight	4	50		
	Drayage		50		
	Commission	6	60	11	60
	Net Proceeds			120	45

No. 1. SEPT. 8, 1881.

Of 10 tubs butter. ACC'T SALES BY LYMAN, SARGENT & CO.

COMMISSION MERCHANT.

Sold by Order and Acc't of BENNETT & RIALE,

Recd. Sept. 2, 1881. OTTAWA, ILL.

Sept.	5	5 tubs, 69½ each, 347½ lbs., at 18c	62	55		
"	8	5 " " " " " " 20c	69	50	132	05
CHARGES:		*Freight*	4	50		
		Drayage		50		
		Commission	6	60	11	60
E. & O. E.		*Net Proceeds*			120	45

VOUCHER.

No. 2. Sept. 3, 1881.

Of 500 bu. potatoes.

For STEWART BROS.

Residence, Elgin, Ill.

1881 Sept. 8	300 bu., at 95c.	285	00		
" 9	200 bu., at 87c.	174	00	459	00
	Freight	12	75		
	Drayage	5	20		
	Commission	22	95	40	90
	Net Proceeds			418	10

No. 2. Sept. 10, 1881.

Of 500 bu. potatoes. } Acc't Sales by Lyman, Sargent & Co.

Commission Merchant.

Sold by Order and Acc't of STEWART BROS.,

Recd. Sept. 3, 1881. Elgin, Ill.

Sept.	8	300 bu., at 95c.	285	00		
"	9	200 " " 87c.	174	00	459	00
Charges:		*Freight*	12	75		
		Drayage	5	20		
		Commission	22	95	40	90
E. & O. E.		***Net Proceeds***			418	10

MANUFACTURING.

The form given in this set will be found practical for many kinds of business.

A list of the sales should be made in the Sales Book, which is posted direct to the Ledger as the entries are journalized in this book.

Keep a Bill Book, Cash Book, Time Book, Journal, Sales Book, and Ledger.

To find amount of cash on hand, add the amount of the footing of the cash column in the S. B. to the Dr. side of the Cash Book, and deduct the footings of the Cr. side.

Carry all cash sales to the Sales Book, and post to the Ledger.

Close the Cash Book whenever the page is full, and carry the balance over to the next page.

Open Cash Book and rule for Sales Book, as shown in this work. Cash sales are entered only in the S. B. All other cash received, or paid out, is entered in the Cash Book.

This form was taken from Furst, Bradley & Co. The Sales Book for this form could be used for wholesaling.

CHICAGO, JAN. 1, 1874.

J. D. Watson, Geo. H. Kendall, and R. T. Crane have this day signed articles of agreement and formed a copartnership, under the style and firm name of Watson, Kendall & Co., to engage in the Manufacturing and Machinist business; parties to invest equal sums, and to share equally in the gains and losses.

2.				
J. D. Watson, Geo. Kendall, and R. T. Crane have this day each invested cash amounting to	50000	00		
3.				
Bot. of W. D. Kerfoot & Co., for cash, building and lot on Desplaines St., 300 ft. by 210, to carry on the above business, for	75750	00		
Dr. Real Estate.				

CHICAGO, JAN. 4, 1874.

Bot. of Crane Brothers Manf'g. Co., one stationary engine, for	12000	00		
Paid cash			7000	00
Our two notes due in 30 and 60 days, $1,500 each			3000	00
Balance on a/c at 90 do.				
Dr. Machinery.				
"				
Paid W. K. Palmer cash for 10 tons coal at $9.50, 5 cords wood at $10				
Dr. Expense.				
5.				
Paid cash for insurance on building and machinery	1275	00		
Dr. Expense.				
6.				
Bot. of Howard & Co., lathes and machinery to carry on the aforesaid business, amounting to			15000	00
Paid cash	5500	00		
Our notes due in 60 and 90 days, for $4,000 each	8000	00		
Balance on a/c				
8.				
Bot. of C. B. Marshall & Co., on a/c iron and steel as per invoice	2750	00		
9.				
Paid Hall & Co. cash for safe			950	00
Dr. Mdse.				

CHICAGO, JAN. 9, 1874.				
Bot. of Geo. W. White, hard wood lumber, as per invoice	765	40		
Paid cash			500	00
Balance on a/c				
10.				
Bot. of R. G. Mason & Co., 4,675 lbs. iron castings at 10c				
Paid our note due in 60 days			300	00
Balance on a/c				
11.				
Accepted C. B. Marshall & Co., draft on us at 30 ds. sight for	1000	00		
"				
Paid H. M. Powell & Co., cash for repairs on house (repairing roof)	275	00		
Dr. Real Estate.				
12.				
Paid J. U. Adams, cash for placing boiler and machinery in proper order, as per contract	950	00		
Dr. Machinery.				
14.				
Bot. of Hall, Kimbark & Co., on a/c iron and steel, as per invoice	1560	90		

CHICAGO, JAN. 15, 1874.

Bot. of Heath & Milligan, paints and oils as per invoice	675	50		
Paid cash			500	00
Balance on a/c at 60 ds.				
Dr. Mdse.				
15.				
Paid T. W. Haas, cash for painting factory, as per contract	450	00		
Dr. Real Estate.				
16.				
Paid J. F. Thompson, cash for printing	260	75		
Dr. Expense.				
17.				
Paid J. W. Jones, cash for blank books and stationery	75	00		
Dr. Expense.				
"				
Paid W. D. Williams, cash for fitting up the office, counters, desks, etc.	675	00		
Dr. Expense.				
19.				
Bot. of J. Blunt & Co., Meridan, Conn., 2,400 lbs. of Sheet Brass at 21¢				
Paid cash			250	00
Balance on a/c				

CHICAGO, JAN. 20, 1874.				
Bot. of Stewart & Aldrich on a/c, 2 bbls. Lard Oil, 43½ gals., each, at 60¢				
Dr. Expense.				
"				
Paid cash to hands as per Time Book	393	75		
Dr. Expense.				
"				
Paid cash for advertising in *Tribune*	21	75		
Dr. Expense.				
22.				
Sold Warder, Mitchell & Co., 6 No. 8 Road Plows at $12 12 No. 21 Peekskill at $9 6 16-in. Sulky at $55 3 18-in. " at $80 6 double Mich. Plows at $30 4 Railroad Plows at $30 Recd. cash	500	00		
Their note at 30 ds. for bal.				
Make this entry in the Sales Book which is written up for January. Use same form for Feb.				
23.				
Sold Cole & Campbell, South Bend, Ind., 12 Furst & Bradley Sulky Rakes at $33 6 12-in. Lawn Rollers at $20 Recd. cash less, 10% discount.				

CHICAGO, JAN. 25, 1874.				
Bot. of Chicago Rolling Mill Co., 21,760 lbs. Pig Iron at 5¢ Paid them our note at 60 ds. Balance on a/c	700	00		
25.				
J. D. Watson drew cash for private use	175	00		
Geo. H. Kendall drew cash	225	00		
26.				
Sold J. C. Nevens & Co., New London, Ind., on a/c at 60 ds. 6 10-in. Prairie Breakers and Colter at $18.50 6 12-in. " " and Colter at $19.50 6 20-in. " " and Colter at $32.00 6 Common Cast Iron Plows at $7.50				
27.				
Paid cash to hands as per Time Book	393	75		
"				
R. F. Crane drew cash for private use	200	00		
29.				
Sold A. P. McDougall, 12 Scratch Harrows at $10 12 Garden Barrows, No. 1, at $5.25 Recd. in paymt. his note Balance on a/c	150	00		

CHICAGO, JAN. 29, 1874.				
Bot. of John Spry, hardwood lumber as per invoice	973	46		
Paid cash			500	00
Our note at 60 ds.			250	00
Balance on a/c at 90 ds.				
30.				
Paid A. Williams, cash for a new side-walk around the factory	172	50		
Dr. Real Estate.				
"				
Bot. of C. N. Holden, on a/c at 90 ds., iron and steel as per invoice	987	45		
31.				
Sold Edwin Hunt & Sons on a/c at 30 ds., Friedman Harrows No. 2,				
12 at $12	144	00		
Post Journal, Sales and Cash Book and take first trial balance, but do not close till manufacturing is finished.				
Feb. 1, 1874.				
Sold Geo. Watson & Co., on a/c at 60 ds.,				
3 Shovel Plows, with Wings, at $6.25				
1 Furst & Bradley Rake	25	00		
6 Sulky Rake Teeth at 60¢				
6 Road Plows at $12				
2.				
Bot. of M. T. Ames & Co.,				
20 tons Hard Coal at $9.25				
5 " Soft " " 6.75				
5 cords Wood " 9.00				
Paid cash			150	00
Bal. on a/c at 30 ds.				

Chicago, Feb. 2, 1874.				
Sold R. M. Marsh & Co., Mendota, Ill.,				
24 Lever Straw Cutters at $5				
12 Mich. Double Plows at $30				
3 12-in. Prairie Breakers at $24				
2 R. R. Plows, very strong, at $30				
1 No. 3 Buffalo Mower	225	00		
Recd. in paymt. their draft on the 3d National Bank of New York	500	00		
Cash	200	00		
Balance on a/c at 60 ds.				
3.				
Paid cash to hands as per Time Book	407	80		
"				
Paid cash for gas bill for Jan.	47	00		
"				
J. D. Watson drew cash for private use	450	00		
R. F. Crane " " " " "	125	00		
4.				
Paid Howard & Co., cash on a/c	700	00		
"				
Sold E. P. Peacock,				
1 Engine and Boiler, with extra attachments, for	3750	00		
Recd. cash			2000	00
His note due in 90 ds.			1000	0C
Balance on a/c				
Cr. Mdse.				

CHICAGO, FEB. 5, 1874.				
Bot. of Brennick & Brown,				
2 pair Draft Horses at $450				
1 Buggy Horse	250	00		
Paid cash			500	00
Balance on a/c at 60 ds.				
Dr. Live Stock.				
6.				
Bot. of Murry Nelson & Co., on a/c,				
1000 bush. Oats at 52¢				
Dr. Expense.				
8.				
Sold Wm. Blair & Co.,				
12 No. 8 Road Plows at $12				
12 Cast Iron Plows at $7				
2 12-inch Lawn Rollers, 16-in., at $20				
2 " " " 30-in., " 38				
6 Blacksmith Anvils, 200 each, at 10¢				
Recd. their note at 30 ds.	300	00		
Balance on a/c				
9.				
Sold H. B. Tanner & Bros., Grand Rapids, Mich.,				
6 Johnson's Reapers at $115				
3 12-in. Lawn Mowers at $20				
Recd. in paymt., cash	250	00		
Their note at 3 months at 10%	300	00		
Balance on a/c				
"				
Paid R. G. Mason & Co., cash on a/c	100	00		
10.				
Paid cash to hands as per Time Book	437	65		

CHICAGO, FEB. 10, 1874.

Bot. of F. B. Stone & Co.,				
2 Double Team Trucks at $750	1500	00		
1 Buggy	275	00		
Paid our note at 90 ds., for	700	00		
Our draft on Wm. Blair & Co., for	100	00		
Cash	500	00		
Balance on a/c at 60 ds.				
Dr. Mdse.				
"				
Paid C. B. Marshall & Co., cash on a/c	500	00		
12.				
Paid H. Haas cash for shoeing horses	12	50		
Dr. Expense.				
"				
Sold W. H. Banks & Co., on a/c at 30 ds.,				
6 No. 3 Lard Presses at $31				
6 No. 2 " " " 20				
3 No. 1 Meat Stuffers " 31				
2 No. 2 " " " 36.50				
Less 15% discount.				
Cr. Mdse. in S. B. for the net amount.				
13.				
Sold Neale & Co, Louisville, Ky.,				
6 No. 1 Hay Cutters at $24				
6 No. 2 " " " 27				
6 No. 3 " " " 32				
Recd in paymt. their note for	300	00		
Balance on a/c at 30 ds.				
14.				
Paid C. B. Marshall & Co., cash for our acceptance	1000	00		

CHICAGO, FEB. 14, 1874.				
Bot. of F. Sturges & Co., on ℅ at 60 ds., a bill of Steel as per invoice	674	83		
15.				
Sold Larrebee & North, Cincinnati, O., 1 34-in. Thresher and Cleaner	330	00		
Recd. their draft on 5th Nat. Bank			250	00
Bal. on ℅ at 60 ds.				
"				
Recd. cash for the draft on the 3d Nat. Bank	500	00		
16.				
Bot. of E. L. Stewart & Co., 1 Machine for Stamping	2750	00		
Paid cash			1000	00
Our notes for 30 ds. and 60 ds., $500 each			1000	00
Balance on ℅ at 60 ds.				
17.				
Paid cash to hands as per Time Book	483	75		
"				
Sold W. A. Pearce & Co., on ℅ at 60 ds., 3 Sulky Attachments at $35	105	00		
"				
Sold S. P. Thompson & Co , Syracuse, N. Y., for cash, 1 No. 2 Thresher complete	585	00		
Less 20% discount				

CHICAGO, FEB. 19, 1874.				
Bot. of T. V. Smith, on a/c 4 tons of Hay at $16 Dr. Expense.				
"				
Paid cash for repairs on factory Dr. Real Estate.	145	00		
"				
Bot. of F. J. Russell, on a/c at 30 ds. 200 Wooden Boxes at 40¢ Dr. Expense.				
"				
Paid Crane Bros. Manf. Co., cash for our note dated Jan. 24, 1874	1500	00		
Pd. cash for interest on the same	11	25		
20.				
Sold Walter Wood, Aurora, Ill., 3 No. 1 Full Iron Warehouse Trucks at $8 3 No 2 Full Iron Warehouse Trucks at $10 3 No. 3 Full Iron Warehouse Trucks at $12.50 3 No. 4 Full Iron Warehouse Trucks at $15 3 No. 5 Full Iron Warehouse Trucks at $20				
Recd. cash	150	00		
Balance on a/c at 60 ds.				
21.				
J. D. Watson drew cash on a/c	275	00		
R. T. Crane " " " "	250	00		
G. H. Kendall " " " "	200	00		

CHICAGO, FEB. 21, 1874.				
Paid Hall, Kimbark & Co., cash on a/c	1000	00		
"				
Bot. of Parkhurst & Wilkinson a bill of Iron and Steel, as per invoice, amounting to	2860	40		
Paid cash			1500	00
Out note for 30 ds.			500	00
Bal. on a/c				
22.				
Recd. of Warder, Mitchell & Co.,				
Cash for their note	550	00		
" " interest on the same	4	58		
"				
Sold Henry Diston & Sons, Philadelphia, Pa.,				
12 No. 1 Sulky Rake at $33				
48 No. 1 " Teeth at 60¢				
6 12-in. Lawn Rollers, 16-in. diam , at $20				
6 12-in. Lawn Rollers, 30-in. diam., at $38				
1 Fieid Roller, 8,760 lbs., at 8½¢ per lb.				
Recd. their draft on W. A. Stone at 10 days' sight, face of draft	750	00		
Their note at 30 ds.	600	00		
Balance on a/c at 90 ds.				
23.				
Bot of the Illinois Iron Foundry,				
7,645 lbs. Iron Castings at 10¢				
Paid our draft on Ed. Hunt & Sons at 10 days' sight for	100	00		
Our note for 60 days	500	00		
Bal. on a/c at 90 days				

CHICAGO, FEB. 23, 1874.

Paid Stewart & Aldrich cash on a/c	52	20		
24.				
Paid cash to hands as per Time Book	490	85		
"				
Bot. of T. McLaughlin on a/c and cash a bill of Hardwood Lumber as per invoice	241	87		
Paid cash			150	00
Bal. on a/c at 60 ds.			91	87
26.				
Sold J. W. Jackson & Co., St. Louis, Mo., at 30 ds., on a/c,				
1 20-in. Cylinder Separator	475	00		
1 Sulky Attachment for Plows	35	00		
"				
Sold S. M. Smith, Madison, Wis., on a/c at 60 ds.,				
1 No. 3 Buffalo Mower	225	00		
27.				
Recd. cash for the draft on the 5th Nat. Bank, Chicago	250	00		
"				
Bot. of A. L. Hale & Bro., on a/c at 60 ds.,				
2 Cylinder Desks at $100				
6 Chairs at $1 50				
Dr. Mdse.				

Chicago, Feb. 28, 1874.				
Sold J. N. Friedman & Co., 12 No. 8 Road Plows with Ex. Points at $12 12 No. 24 Road Plows, Common Points, at $7 3 16-in. Sulky Plows at $55 6 No. 2 Sod Plows, 14-in. cut, at $18 6 No. 4 Hay Cutters, 2 Knives, at $45 6 No. 5 " " 1 Knife, " 40 1 Climax Mower and Reaper	200	00		
1 Field Roller, 7,000 lbs., at 8½¢				
Recd. in paymt. their draft on Good & Co.,			1000	00
Their note for 60 ds.			500	00
Bal. on a/c at 90 ds.				
"				
Paid Murry Nelson & Co., cash on a/c	300	00		
"				
Recd. of J. McDougall, Cash for his note	150	00		
" " interest on the same		75		
"				
Bot. of Blake, Whitehouse & Co., 100 tons Ind. Block Coal at $4.10				
Paid our note at 30 ds. for			200	00
Cash			100	00
Balance on a/c				
Dr. Expense. **Close Cash and Sales Book and take first Trial Balance.**				
March 1, 1874.				
Sold E. W. Brown & Co., for cash, 6 No. 1 Half Iron Warehouse Trucks at $7 Less 10% discount.				

CHICAGO, MARCH 1, 1874.

Sold J. L. Wayne & Son, at 30 ds. on a/c, 6 No. 1 Meat Stuffers at $31 6 No. 2 " " " 36.50 Less 25% discount.				
"				
Paid F. V. Smith cash on a/c	50	00		
2.				
Paid M. T. Ames cash on a/c	100	00		
"				
Bot. of Stewart, Aldrich & Co., on a/c, 4 bbls. Lard Oil, 43 gal. each, at 60¢				
"				
Sold E. P. Peacock, 1 small Engine 1 extra Boiler Recd. cash Bal. on a/c at 60 ds.	 600 75 500	 00 00 00	 675	 00
"				
Paid cash for gas bill for February	21	60		
"				
Bot. of C. Marchant on a/c, 50 Bush. Corn at 70¢ **Dr. Expense.**				
"				
Paid Howard & Co. cash for our note, their favor	4000	00		

Chicago, March 2, 1874.

Sold W. A. Drew & Co., Bloomington, Ill., 6 No. 1 Peekskill Plows at $9 6 No. 3 " " " 7 50 3 Michigan Plows (double) at $30 3 Furst & Bradley Sulky Rakes at $33 36 " " " Teeth at 60¢ Recd. their note at 10 ds. Bal. on a/c	200	00		
7.				
Accepted C. B. Marshall's draft at 30 days for	500	00		
8.				
Sold Jas. A. Davidson, McGregor, Iowa, on a/c, 1 Lawn Roller, 4,000 lbs., at 8½¢				
"				
Sold R. Fisher & Co., Dayton, Ohio, at 60 ds., 12 Lever Straw Cutters at $5.25				
9.				
Recd. of Wm. Blair & Co. Cash for their note, our favor	200	00		
Interest on same	1	00		
"				
Paid Heath & Milligan cash on a/c	100	00		

CHICAGO, MARCH 10, 1874.

Sold White & Russell, Plymouth, Ind., 6 Friedman Harrows, 9 ft., at $12 6 " " 12 " " 18 6 Common Cast Iron Plows " 7 3 No. 1 Full Iron Trucks " 8 3 No. 2 " " " " 10 3 No. 3 " " " " 12.50 3 No. 4 " " " " 15 1 No. 8, two knives, Hay Cutter Recd. their note at 60 ds. for Bal. on a/c at 90 ds.	140	00	350	00
"				
Recd. cash of H. B. Tanner & Bro., on a/c	100	00		
"				
Paid cash to hands as per Time Book	501	10		
12.				
J. D. Watson drew cash for private use	145	00		
R. F. Crane " " " " "	250	00		
Geo. H. Kendall " " " " "	75	00		
"				
Recd. cash of W. H. Banks & Co., on a/c	300	00		
13.				
Sold S. P. Jones, Zanesville, Ohio, on a/c at 30 ds., 1 Climax Mower and Reaper	200	00		
"				
Paid R. G. Mason & Co., Cash for our note " " interest	300 3	00 00		
"				
Recd. cash of Neale & Co., on a/c	100	00		

CHICAGO, MARCH 13, 1874.				
Paid Howard & Co., cash on a/c	300	00		
14.				
Recd. cash for H. Diston's draft on W. A. Stone, our favor	750	00		
"				
Paid cash for repairs on factory Dr. Real Estate.	225	00		
"				
Bot. of John Alston & Co., on a/c, a bill of Paints and Oils, per invoice Dr. Mdse.	185	40		
"				
Bot. of D. M. Ford & Co.,				
8,900 lbs. Iron Castings at 9¢				
Paid our draft on J. W. Jackson & Co.	300	00		
Our note at 30 ds.	200	00		
Balance on a/c				
15.				
Recd. cash for J. N. Friedman & Co.'s draft on S. M. Good, our favor	1000	00		
"				
Sold E. S. Wood, Benton Harbor, Mich., on a/c at 60 ds.,				
1 Sulky Attachment for Plow	35	00		
"				
J. D. Watson drew cash for private use	150	00		
R. T. Crane drew cash	100	00		
16.				
Sold L. J. Wentworth, Joliet, Ill.,				
1 Boiler and Engine complete, as per contract			9000	00
Recd. cash	5000	00		
Balance on a/c	4000	00		

CHICAGO MARCH 16, 1874.

Geo. Kendall drew cash for private use			250	00
"				
Paid E. L. Stewart & Co. cash for our note	500	00		
17.				
Sold F. W. Baker & Co.,				
1 No. 2 Thresher, complete with all Attachments	585	00		
1 Lawn Roller	123	00		
1 Mich. Double Plow	30	00		
Recd. their acceptance at 15 ds. sight			500	00
Balance on a/c at 30 ds.				
"				
Paid cash to hands as per Time Book	486	40		
19.				
Paid F. J. Russell cash on a/c	50	00		
"				
Bot. of James Goodwill & Co., on a/c,				
150 Boxes, as per order,	96	00		
Dr Expense.				
"				
Bot. of Hubbard & Spencer,				
1 Grinding Stone	45	00		
3 Kegs Nails at $5	15	00		
1 Lot of Tools, as per invoice,	140	00		
Paid cash	100	00		
Bal. on a/c at 60 ds.				
20.				
Sold R. G. Trust on a/c at 60 ds.				
1 Extra Sulky Plow	80	00		
"				
Paid Parkhurst & Wilkinson,				
Cash for our note	500	00		
" " interest	5	00		

Chicago, March 21, 1874.				
Sold J. I. Bradley & Co., on a/c,				
1 Engine for Threshing Machine	475	00		
"				
J. D. Watson drew cash for private use	175	00		
"				
Recd. of J. C. Nevens, cash on a/c	200	00		
22.				
Recd. of H. Diston & Sons,				
Cash for their note	600	00		
" " interest	3	00		
"				
Recd. of E. P. Peacock cash on a/c	150	00		
23.				
Sold J. McKenna & Co.,				
1 20-in. Cylinder Separator	475	00		
1 No. 3 Buffalo Mower	225	00		
Recd. their note	200	00		
Cash	300	00		
Balance on a/c	200	00		
"				
Geo. H. Kendall drew cash for private use	140	00		
24.				
Paid cash to hands	491	84		
"				
R. T. Crane drew cash	100	00		
Inventory of unsold property,				
Machinery,	30700	00		
Live Stock,	1150	00		
Real Estate,	77017	50		
Merchandise,	6940	71		

SALES BOOK FOR MANUFACTURING.

The Sales Book is given for January, only, as a guide. February and March are to be written up on the same plan. When the page is full carry over the footings to the next, and credit mdse. once a month when a trial balance is taken. The first two columns will balance the mdse. column.

CHICAGO, JAN. 22, 1874.					
L. Fol.			Sunds. *Dr.*	Cash. *Dr.*	Mdse. *Cr.*
	Bills rec.		550 00		
	Cash			500 00	
	Warder Mitchell & Co.,				
	6 No. 8 Road Plows at $12,	$ 72.00			
	12 No. 21 Peekskill Plows at $9,	108.00			
	6 16-in. Sulky Plows at $55,	330.00			
	3 18-in. " " " 80,	240.00			
	6 Double Mich. Plows at $30,	180.00			
	4 Railroad Plows at $30,	120.00			1050 00
	23.				
	Cash			464 40	
	Cole & Campbell, less dis.				
	12 Furst & Bradley's Sulky Rakes at $33,	$396.00			464 40
	6 12-in. Lawn Rollers at $20,	120.00			
	26.				
	J. C. Nevens & Co., on ac't,		465 00		
	6 10-in. Prairie Breakers at $18.50,	$111.00			
	6 12-in. " " " 19.50,	117.00			
	6 20-in. " " " 32.00,	192.00			465 00
	6 Common Cast Iron " 7.50,	45.00			
	29.				
	Bills rec.		150 00		
	W. P. McDougall		33 00		
	12 Scratch Harrows at $10.00,	$120.00			183 00
	12 Garden Barrows " 5.25,	63.00			
	31.				
	Edwin Hunt & Sons, on ac't,		144 00		
	12 Friedman Harrows at $12,	$144.00			144 00
			1342 00	964 40	2306 40

TIME BOOK.

The following Time Book can be used, and the balance of the am't due hands carried out in this book. By this method it is not necessary to open an account with the hands in the Ledger. The columns can be extended for one month or more in business.

1874		Week Ending Jan. 20.											Week Ending Jan. 27.									
Names.	Wages per Day.	Monday.	Tuesday.	Wednesday.	Thursday.	Friday.	Saturday.	Wages for the Week.	Former Balance Due.	Total Amount Due.	Amount Paid.	Balance Due.	Monday.	Tuesday.	Wednesday.	Thursday.	Friday.	Saturday.	Wages for the Week.	Total Amount Due.	Amount Paid.	Balance Due.
John Doyle......	2 00	1	1	1	1	1	1	12 00	5 00	17 00	10 00	7 00	1	1		1	1	1	10 00	17 00	15 00	2 00
Wm. Watson.....	1 75	1		1	1	1	1	8 75	3 00	11 75	10 00	1 75	1	1	1	1	1	1	10 50	12 25	10 00	2 25
Chas. Davis......	2 25	1	1	1	1	1	1	13 50	4 50	18 00	12 00	6 00	1	1	1	1			9 00	15 00	13 00	2 00
John Smith.....	2 00	1	1		1	1	1	10 00		10 00	10 00		1	1	1	1	1	1	12 00	12 00	10 00	2 00
Geo. Jones	1 75	1	½	1		1	1	7 88	2 00	9 88	9 88		1	1	1	1	1	1	10 50	10 50	10 00	50
P. Ryan.........	2 00		1	1	1	1	1	10 00	1 50	11 50	10 00	1 50	1	1	1	1	1	1	12 00	13 50	12 00	1 50
Chas. Rowell.....	2 25	1	1	1	1	1	1	13 50		13 50	12 00	1 50	1			1	1	1	9 00	10 50	10 50	
James Williams..	1 50		1	1	1	1	½	6 75		6 75	5 00	1 75	1	1	1	1	1	1	9 00	10 75	10 75	
C. B. Thompson.	1 75	1	1	1		1	1	8 75		8 75	8 75		1	1	1	1	1	1	10 50	10 50	10 50	
Geo. Davis.......	1 25	1	1	1	1			5 00	5 00	10 00	8 00	2 00	1	1	1	1	1	1	7 50	9 50	8 00	1 50
A. D. Howard...	2 00	1	1	1	1	1	1	12 00		12 00	12 00		1	1	1				6 00	6 00	6 00	
H. Burnham....	2 00	1	1		1	1	1	10 00		10 00	10 00		1	1	1	1	1	1	12 00	12 00	12 00	
J. Carqueville....	1 75	1	1	1	1	1	1	10 50	5 00	15 50	10 00	5 50	1	1	1	1	1	1	10 50	16 00	15 00	1 00

INVOICES.

To become proficient in making out invoices requires practice and rapid and correct extensions. By extensions we refer to the carrying out the price of each article.

We give quite a number of exercises, some of which were taken from the Chicago houses.

The amount of invoices are not given, for it is better for the student to find the correct extensions and footings of each in the same manner as he would in a mercantile house or an office.

No bill clerk can become an expert from the practice obtained from any arithmetic ever published; the exercises are too few and simple. Correct calculations should be made on all the following invoices.

Carry each extension in the first column and write the footings in the second on the same line as the last item.

In some houses the invoices are written with copying ink and impressions taken with a press, in a book called the sale book, and posted direct to ledger.

No. 3.		
CHICAGO, Sept. 13, 1882.		
THOS. SPENCER.		
Bot. of WM. ATKINSON.		
15 yds. Broadcloth at $2.75		
18 " Cassimere at 95¢		
25 " Drilling at 13¢		
15 doz spools Cotton Thread at 56¢		
12½ yds. Gingham at 23¢		
42¾ yds. Fine Muslin at 18½¢		
12 yds. Red Flannel at 62¢		
22¾ yds Silk Velvet at $4.25		
15 gross Shirt Buttons at 72¢		
12 doz. Wool Hose at $2.75		
8 prs. Kid Gloves at $1 12½		
5 doz Linen Napkins at $2.20		
4 doz. Shirt Bosoms at $2.25		
1 doz Silk Handkerchiefs at 87¢		
16 yds. Velvet Ribbon at 22¢		
18 " Sheeting at 17¢		
28 " Prints at 13¢		
Less 5% Dis.		
Paid. WM. ATKINSON.		

No. 4.

CHICAGO, Sept. 20, 1882.

WM. B. COOK.

Bot. of SPRAGUE WARNER & CO.

3 hhds. Sugar, 1450 lbs. each, at 7¼¢
7 chests Green Tea, 65¾ lbs. each, at 52¢
14 " Black " 62 lbs. each, at 43¢
13 sacks Rio Coffee, 75 lbs. each, at 28¢
12 " Java " 68 " " at 31⅓¢
7 bbls. A Sugar, 205 lbs. each, at 7¼¢
4 hhds. Molasses, 63 gals. each, at 43¢
2 hhds. Prunes, 1162 lbs. and 1324 lbs., at 7¾¢
Less 2½% for cash.

Find the net cost and receipt the invoice.

No. 5.

CHICAGO, Sept. 25, 1882.

D. O. MILLER.

Bot. of GARDNER & SPRY.

5768 Brick at $7.87 M.
15725 ft. Pine Lumber at $5.75 M.
9726 ft. Maple " at $45.20 M.
235 ft. Black Walnut at $65.00 M.
1462 ft. Hard Pine at $8.75 C.
6728 lbs. Hay at $9.75 per ton

Make D. O. Miller's note due Gardner & Spry for 60 days from date for amount of invoice, interest 7%.

No. 6.

CHICAGO, Sept. 14, 1882.

MRS. SARAH PRESTON.

Bot. of GEO. SHERWOOD & CO.

50 Model 1st Rds., 32¢
36 " 2nd " 37¢
42 " 3rd " 58¢
26 " 4th " 96¢
100 Student's 1st Rds., 16¢
75 " 2nd " 25¢

20 Students' 3rd Rds., 40¢
20 " 4th " 75¢
19 " 5th " 85¢
47 Analytical Spellers, 18¢
20 doz. Analytical No. 1 Copy Bks., $1.00
20 " " " 1½ " 1.00
20 " " " 2 " 1.00
20 " " " 2½ " 1.00
24 " " " 3 " 1.00
22 " " " 3½ " 1.00
19 " " " 4 " 1.00
13 " " " 5 " 1.00
14 " " " 6 " 1.00
19 " " " 7 " 1.00
Less 10%.

No. 7.

CHICAGO, Sept. 14, 1882.

S. A. MAXWELL & Co.

Bot. of GEO. SHERWOOD & Co.

33 doz. Five Cent Writing Spellers, 48¢
19½ doz. 4 col. " " 72¢
44¾ " 6 " " " 85¢
19¼ " 6 " Interleaved Writing Spellers, $1.00
22 doz. Five Cent. Spelling Lesson Blanks, 48¢
18 1-6 doz. Ten Cent " " " 90¢
7 set Model Reading Charts, $3.00
11 set Analytical Writing Charts, $2.25
11 doz. Part I. Students' Series, 54¢
49 Part 18, Students' Series, 20¢
700 Analytical Copy Book Covers, per hundred, $1.15
99 doz. Babbittonian Copy Books, $1.00
41½ doz. Penmanship Practice Blanks, $1.00
46 Peries Example Books, 8¢
19 doz. Sherwood's Registers, $8.40
4 doz Payne's Class Books, $6.24
3½ doz. Kitchen and Dining Room Bk., $2.40
4½ " Drew's Book-Keeping, $18.00
1 1-6 doz. sets Drew's Blanks, $24.00
3 doz. each Part 4, 5, 6, 7 and 8 Students' Series, 54¢ per doz.

Less 12¾%

No. 8.

CHICAGO, Sept. 14, 1882

W. W. WILKINS.

Bot. of GEO. SHERWOOD & Co.

10 doz. Pen and Pencil Copy Books, No. 1, 45¢
9 " " " " " Nol 2, 45¢
10 " Elementary Copy Book, No. 1, 65¢
9 " " " " No. 2, 65¢
8 " " " " No. 3, 65¢
7 " " " " No. 4, 65¢
4 " " " " No. 5, 65¢
25 Analytical 1st Rds., 20¢
40 " 2nd " 32¢
25 " 3rd " 50¢
10 " Intermediate, 55¢
9 " 4th Rds., 63¢
8 " 5th " 85¢
18 " 6th " 96¢
83 Model History, 80¢
46 Drew's Book-Keeping, $1.50
43 set Drew's Book-Keeping Blanks, $2.00
84 Model Arith., 95¢
41 " Elementary, 55¢
19 " 1st Arith., 40¢
41 " 2nd " 45¢
39 " 3rd " 45¢
Less 7½%.

No. 9.

CHICAGO, Oct. 1, 1882.

D. MCDOUGALL.

Bot. of WESTERN NEWS CO.

7 reams Ledger Paper, 12 lbs. each, at 28¢
13 " Broad Bill, 11 lbs., at 28¢
7 " Foolscap, 12 lbs., at 26¢
8 " Com. Note, 10 lbs., at 28¢
7 M. Envelopes, at $3.60, less 15%
5 gross Penholders, at $6.25, less 18%
3 " Pencils, at $5.75, less 30%
12 " Worthington's Black Ink, at $8.50, less 15%
6 " 2 oz. Carmine at $6.50, less 12½%
2½ doz. Ruling Pens, at $6.25, less 40%

3 doz. Pocket Knives, at \$3.25		
4 " " " at \$4 50		
12 gross Spencerian Pens, No. 1, at \$1.05		
7 " Gillott's " No. 303, at \$1.00		
4 doz Ink Stands, at \$1.20		
Less 5% for cash.		
Paid.		

STATEMENTS.

Accountants are often required to make statements of a customer's account in which he itemizes the Debits and Credits and strikes a balance. Find the balance of the following statement:

STATEMENT No. 1.

CHICAGO, Aug. 10, 1882.

J. F. KING,

In ℅ with P. L. MORTON.

1882.

Jan.	1	To 245 lbs. Sugar at 8½¢		
"	5	" 7 " Tea at 43¢		
Feb.	9	" 18 " Rio Coffee at 27¢		
"	15	" 37 " Java " at 31¢		
Mar.	12	" 2 sacks Flour at \$3.75		
Apr.	20	" 5 gal. Molasses at 40¢		
May	10	" 100 lbs. Butter Crackers at 9¢		
June	15	" 50 " Pearl Starch at 12½¢		
July	3	" 10 " Golden Syrup at 70¢		
"	10	" 3 " Spice at 20¢		
"	20	" 5 " Ginger at 18¢		
"	25	" 28 " Dried Peaches at 12½¢		
Aug.	10	" 56 " Mackerel at 8¾¢.		
		CR.		
June	10	By 2 firkins Butter, 56 lbs. each, at 14¢		
Feb.	15	" Cash	12	50
"	20	" 7 bush. Potatoes at 75¢		
Mar.	1	" Cash	8	75
June	1	" 3 Tons of Hay at \$2.30 per ton.		
		Balance due		

STATEMENT NO. 2.

BOSTON, Jan. 1, 1881.

W. H. GOODWIN,

Bot. of MARSHALL FIELD & Co.

1881.

July	7	To 25 yds. Cambric at 9¢		
"	7	" 50 " Print at 11½¢		
"	7	" 13 " Cassimere at $1.25		
"	20	" 20 " Sheeting at 11¢		
"	20	" 13¼ yds. Broadcloth at $3.75		
"	20	" 5¾ " Velvet at $2.87½¢		
Aug.	20	" 25 yds. French Print at 16⅔¢		
"	20	" 18 " Lyonese at 62¢		
		CR.		
Sept.	1	By 45 bush. Coal at 11¢		
"	7	" 7 cords of Wood at $3.75		
Oct.	15	" Cash	12	00
"	25	" 9 days' Labor at $2.00		
		Balance due		
		Received payment.		

BUSINESS CORRESPONDENCE.

There is no feature of a business education more important than correspondence. To be able to write a well formed letter, couched in language clear and concise, to enable the writer to fully express all the subjects intended, requires no ordinary skill.

Brevity should constitute one of the elements of a business letter. Say what you have to say briefly as possible, and yet present all the points clearly.

Punctuation, correct spelling, the proper use of capital letters, paragraphing, and grammatical construction, should receive due attention.

We give a few models to serve as a guide to beginners, yet the student should not stop when all of these are copied.

An excellent practice is for the teacher to divide the school into two classes, each individual student to write to some member of the school, to be answered by the pupil receiving the letter. The letters received should be criticised, and note the corrections when read. By this method the more advanced pupils will assist those more backward, who will soon learn to imitate the best letters in style and composition.

The author has introduced this method with the most favorable results in his business colleges during the past fifteen years.

Directions for Writing a Business Letter.

1st. Commence on the first line about the center, and give the residence and date.

2nd. Write the name of the person or firm to whom the letter is addressed on the second line, at the left, three-fourths of an inch from the edge of the paper, and the residence on the third line directly below the name addressed.

3rd. Dear Sir for persons or Gentlemen for firms are usually written on the fourth line, a little to right of name and residence.

4th. Leave a uniform margin on the left of three-fourths of an inch between writing and the edge of the paper, and increase this space to one and one-half inches when a new paragraph is commenced.

5th. Use your taste in closing a letter. Yours truly, Truly yours, Respectfully yours, Yours, etc., are the most common.

6th. Sign your name to the right, on the line below the ending of the letter.

7th. Punctuate and read carefully before enclosing the letter in the envelope.

Superscription of the Letter.

Persons not accustomed to direct letters usually find it difficult to write on a line parallel with the envelope. The following directions may assist the writer.

Place your envelope in such a position that the pen will pass directly over the center of it from left to right, and by keeping the arm and envelope in this position the desired superscription can be produced. Write town or city below the name to the right, and state still lower the State.

No. 1.

Elgin, Ill., Sept. 4, 1882.

Worthington & Drew,

Gentlemen,—Wishing to attend a Business College, I write requesting information relative to terms, branches taught, etc.

What is the average time required to complete a thorough business course of instruction for a young man possessing a common school education?

Do you guarantee situations for your graduates?

Please write what good board can be obtained for per week in private families, also the expense for books and blanks for the entire course.

Very truly yours,

J. D. Hamilton.

No. 2.

Lakeside Business College,
Chicago, Sept. 4, 1882

J. D. Hamilton,
Dear Sir,

We are in receipt of your favor of the 4th inst., and we mail you, as per your request, our catalogue, circulars, etc., giving you full information relative to our College.

We do not guarantee situations to our graduates, but give our influence to worthy students. Merchandise and services will always bring the market value, and our students who have heretofore passed the prescribed course of study at this institution have been very successful in obtaining positions.

Trusting that we may have the pleasure of receiving a call from you, we are, Very respectfully yours,

WORTHINGTON & DREW.
81 No. Clark St., Chicago.

No. 3.

A MILD DUNNING LETTER.

Chicago, Sept. 8, 1882.

W. E. Raymond,
Aurora, Ill.,

Dear Sir,—Inclosed please find a statement of your account. The balance due me I find to be $125.50, and as I have some heavy invoices to meet on the 15th inst., a remittance per draft, for the above amount, on or before the 12th, will do me a great favor.

Hoping that you will find it convenient to comply with my request, and that you will favor me with your orders for goods in the future, as in the past, I remain as ever,

Very truly yours,
GEO. H. DANIELS.

No. 4.

ANSWER TO NO. 3.

Aurora, Ills., Sept. 10, 1882.

Geo. H. Daniels,

Dear Sir,—Your favor of the 9th was this day received, and I inclose draft for $125.50, the balance due you as per statement.

Pardon me for not remitting before, but business has been so pressing the past two weeks that I really did not find time to examine your account.

Rest assured that I shall continue to patronize your house, as my orders have always been promptly and satisfactorily filled. Thanking you for past favors, I remain

Yours truly,

E. W. RAYMOND.

No 5.

LETTER APPLYING FOR A POSITION.

Chicago, Sept. 7, 1882.

Tribune Office, A 59,

Dear Sir,—In answer to your Ad. in yesterday's *Tribune* wanting a bill clerk, I respectfully offer my services. I was employed in the house of J. V. Farwell & Co. for two years, as bill clerk, and owing to a severe attack of sickness was obliged to give up my position last July.

Having fully recovered my health and wishing for employment, I enclose references from the above well-known firm.

An answer granting an interview will meet with prompt attention.

Very respectfully,

D. H. HUDSON,
81 No. Clark St., Chicago

No. 6.

ANSWER TO A LETTER INQUIRING FOR PRICE LIST.

Chicago, Sept. 14, 1882.

Mr. Henry C. Adams,
Milwaukee, Wis.,

Dear Sir,

I hand you herewith enclosed a price list of the celebrated Writing Inks in accordance with your request of the 12th inst.

These inks are unequalled for fine penmanship or for school use.

Hoping to receive your order, I am,

Very truly yours,

B. M. WORTHINGTON.

No. 7.

LETTER OF INTRODUCTION.

Boston, Sept. 4, 1882.

Marshall Field & Co.,
Chicago, Ill.,

Gentlemen,—This will introduce you to Mr. C. B. Walker, the bearer, a young man of good character and habits of industry and integrity.

He has been employed in our house during the past four years as an accountant and correspondent, during which time we have found him correct and trustworthy.

He visits Chicago with the intention of making that city his home.

Any favors you can show him by giving him employment, or in assisting him in getting a situation elsewhere, will be considered a personal favor to us.

Very truly yours,
JORDAN, MARSH & CO.

No. 8.

Chicago, Sept. 15, 1882

E. T. Edwards & Co.,
389 Market St., San Francisco, Cal.,
Gentlemen,

At the request of Mr. J. H. Reynolds with F. B. McAvoy & Co., of this city, I send you by this mail samples of Upholstery Goods, and also Illustrated Catalogue of Furniture.

I would be pleased to receive your orders for goods in this line, and respectfully submit the following discounts, which I trust will be found satisfactory:

No. 446 Suite, quality "A," Plush, 25 %.
" " " " "B," " 28 %.
" 349 " " "A 1," " 20 %.
" " " " "C," Spun Silk, 15 %.

All other styles in catalogue 20 and 5%. Terms, 60 days net; less 3% 30 days.

In quoting the above, I have taken into consideration the quantity of goods you handle, and have accordingly based prices upon C/L Lots.

Should you, however, feel disinclined to order in that quantity before first examining the goods, I would be pleased to send you samples, upon approval, of the various grades, which you may hold, subject to my order, should they not prove satisfactory to you.

Hoping to receive your favors.

Yours respectfully,
W. H. GOODROW,
Per H.

FORMS FOR BUSINESS PAPER.

SIGHT DRAFT.

$500. CHICAGO, July 21, 1873.

At sight, pay Alonzo Spicer, or order, Five Hundred Dollars, and charge to the account of

To SHERWOOD & CO.,
145 Broadway, N. Y. W. A. DREW.

TIME DRAFT ACCEPTED.

$75. CHICAGO, July 21, 1873.

At ten days sight, pay H. C. Smith, or order, Seventy-five Dollars, and charge to the account of

To JONES & CO.,
Boston. WM. GOODRICH.

Accepted across the face as follows: "Accepted July 23, 1873.
"JONES & CO."

INDIVIDUAL PROMISSORY NOTE.

$300.75. CHICAGO, July 21, 1873.

Thirty days after date, I promise to pay Geo. O. Hudson, or order, Three Hundred Dollars and Seventy-five Cents, with interest at ten per cent. per annum. Value received.

GEO. PEABODY

JOINT AND SEVERAL NOTE.

$800. CHICAGO, July 1. 1873.

Three months after date, we, jointly and severally, promise to pay R. C. Moore, or order, Eight Hundred Dollars, with interest at ten per cent. per annum; payable at the Second National Bank, Chicago. Value received.

CHAS. SIMPSON,
RICHARD JACKSON.

Principal and Surety Note.

$100. Chicago, July 22, 1873.

Thirty days after date, I promise to pay John Richardson, or order, One Hundred Dollars, with interest at ten per cent. per annum. Value Received.

W. A. Drew, Principal.
James Williams, Surety.

Chattel Note.

$300. Chicago, July 21, 1873.

Three months from date, value received, I promise to pay Daniel Drew, or order, Three Hundred Dollars, in wheat at the then market rate, the same to be delivered as per his order, in the city of Chicago.

Simon Still, Jr.

Promissory Note not Negotiable.

$75. Chicago, July 21, 1873.

Thirty days after date, I promise to pay W. A. Drew Seventy-five Dollars, at the office of Drew's Business College, 278 W. Madison Street.

Saml. J. Kline.

Due Bill Drawing Interest.

$25. Chicago, July 21, 1873.

Due H. C. Kendall on demand, Twenty-five Dollars, with interest from date.

W. A. Spencer.

For Mdse. Without Interest.

$300. Chicago, July 21, 1873.

Due John Jones, or order, Three Hundred Dollars, payable in corn on the first day of October next, at the then market price. Value received.

Joseph Munson.

ORDERS.

To Apply on Account.

St. Louis, July 25, 1873.

Mr. Chas. Jones,

Please pay bearer Twenty-five Dollars in merchandise from your store, and charge the same to my account.

Edwin Forrest.

In Full on Account.

Chicago, July 21, 1873.

Hamlin, Hale & Co.,

Please pay to John Wilson, or bearer, Seventy-five Dollars in goods from your store, and this shall be a receipt in full of my account.

C. E. Johnson.

RECEIPTS.

On Account.

$50.

Received, Chicago, July 25, 1873, of John Smith, Fifty Dollars, on account.

Geo. R. Davis.

In Full of all Demands.

Received, Chicago, July 21, 1873, of Samuel Richards, Seventy-five Dollars, in full of all demands.

Hiram M. Drew.

To Apply on Contract.

$700. Chicago, July 1, 1873.

Received of Wm. Allen, Seven Hundred Dollars, the same to apply on contract for building house at No. 540 W. Madison Street.

John King.

RECEIPT FOR PROPERTY.

CHICAGO, July 21, 1873.

Received of John Druitt one Rosewood Piano, to be held in trust for him and returned on his demand.

A. SPICER.

TO APPLY AS INDORSEMENT.

Received, Chicago, July 21, 1873, Fifty Dollars, on the within note.

S. C. DRUMMOND.

CHECK ON A BANK, PAYABLE TO BEARER.

$90.

First National Bank pay Saml. Watson, or bearer, Ninety Dollars,

No. 246. W. E. FRENCH.

PAYABLE TO ORDER.

$50 CHICAGO, July 21, 1873.

First National Bank,

Pay L. Buzzell, cr order,

Fifty Dollars.

No. 247. W. E. FRENCH.

CERTIFICATE OF DEPOSIT.

NEW YORK, July 21, 1873.

Second National Bank,

R. H. Drew has deposited in this Bank, One Thousand Dollars, payable to his order on return of this Certificate.

JOHN SMITH, Teller.

www.ingramcontent.com/pod-product-compliance
Lightning Source LLC
LaVergne TN
LVHW021406110826
845150LV00007B/1804

* 9 7 8 1 4 2 5 5 1 2 0 5 7 *